PAUL AND SCRIPTURE

PAUL AND SCRIPTURE

STEVE MOYISE

𝕭

Baker Academic

a division of Baker Publishing Group
Grand Rapids, Michigan

© 2010 by Steve Moyise

Published in North America by Baker Academic
a division of Baker Publishing Group
P.O. Box 6287, Grand Rapids, MI 49516-6287
www.bakeracademic.com

ISBN 978-0-8010-3924-9

Published by an arrangement with SPCK
36 Causton Street
London SW1P 4ST

Printed in the United States of America

Library of Congress Cataloging-in-Publication Data is on file at the Library of Congress, Washington, DC.

Unless otherwise noted, Scripture quotations are taken from the New Revised Standard Version (NRSV) of the Bible, Anglicized Edition, copyright © 1989, 1995 by the Division of Christian Education of the National Council of the Churches of Christ in the USA. Used by permission. All rights reserved.

Scripture quotations from the Revised Standard Version (RSV) of the Bible are copyright © 1946, 1952 and 1971 by the Division of Christian Education of the National Council of the Churches of Christ in the USA. Used by permission. All rights reserved. NB The RSV Apocrypha was copyright © 1957.

Contents

Contents

Contents

Abbreviations

JB	The Jerusalem Bible
JSOT	*Journal for the Study of the Old Testament*
JSOTSup	Journal for the Study of the Old Testament Supplement
KJV	King James Version
LXX	Septuagint (Greek translation)
MT	Masoretic Text (standard version of the Hebrew Bible)
NETS	New English Translation of the Septuagint
NIV	New International Version
NJB	New Jerusalem Bible
NRSV	New Revised Standard Version
RSV	Revised Standard Version
SBL	Society of Biblical Literature
SBLDS	Society of Biblical Literature Dissertation Series
WUNT	Wissenschaftliche Untersuchungen zum Neuen Testament

Introduction

Many church debates involve a particular interpretation of Scripture, and many will at some point quote from the letters of St Paul. In most cases this is to quote the conclusions that Paul reached as he himself wrestled with the meaning of those texts that Christians call the Old Testament and Jews the Tanak or Hebrew Bible. There are over 100 explicit quotations of Scripture in Paul's letters and at least double that number of allusions. However, what is potentially more useful than just citing Paul's answers to first-century questions is to study *how* Paul interpreted Scripture, and that is the theme of this book. Paul believed that the Scriptures were the very 'oracles of God' (Rom. 3.2) and thus carried supreme authority in all matters. However, he had also come to believe that the divine plan revealed in Scripture had taken a significant step forward in the coming of Jesus Christ and the birth of the Church. There are still things to come (1 Cor. 15.20–28), but it is what has been fulfilled in the Christ-event – a convenient way of describing the life, death and resurrection of Christ and the birth of the Church – that is decisive for Paul. This revelation caused Paul to look at the Scriptures with new eyes, sometimes clarifying what was written and sometimes reinterpreting it. This interaction between old and new goes by many names, among them dialogical, reflexive, intertextual, and lies at the heart of all interpretation. How can Scripture 'speak' to new situations?

There are 13 letters in the New Testament that bear Paul's name and it is common to divide them into three groups. The first group is known as the 'undisputed' letters. These are mainly from the early period of Paul's life (*c.* 49–55 CE) and are accepted as genuine by the majority of scholars. There is debate as to whether 1 Thessalonians or Galatians is the earliest, followed by the two letters to the Corinthians and Romans. Philippians was written from prison, perhaps in this period or perhaps in the period narrated by Acts 28. The short personal letter to Philemon makes up the total of seven 'undisputed' letters. A second group (Colossians and Ephesians) appears to come from a slightly later period. These letters exhibit a more developed understanding of the Church as the body of Christ (Col. 1.15–20; Eph. 4.1–16) and show signs of what later theologians would call church polity or organization (Col. 3.18—4.1; Eph. 5.21–33). Scholarship is evenly divided as to whether these come directly from Paul's hand or were written in his name. The third group is known as the Pastoral Epistles, written to church leaders (Timothy and Titus) and containing instructions for the appointment of bishops (*episkopoi*), deacons (*diakonoi*) and elders (*presbyteroi*) in the Church. This is very different from the 'charismatic' leadership of the early house churches (e.g. 1 Cor. 12—14), but there is dispute about how late their period is. The majority of scholars think that they belong to a period of around 80–100 CE and that they were written by one of Paul's disciples. Others suggest that the imprisonment of Acts 28 did not result in Paul's death and that after his release he engaged in several years of missionary work (perhaps fulfilling the wish expressed in Romans 15.24 to get to Spain); he was then imprisoned a second time and it was at this point that he wrote the Pastoral Epistles. Finally, we should mention 2 Thessalonians, which differs so much from 1 Thessalonians that many scholars find it difficult to accept that it comes directly from Paul's hand. Other scholars, however, do not find the differences insurmountable.

These various arguments are complex and need not detain us, for in fact the majority of Paul's quotations come from the undisputed letters. The figures set out in the simple table opposite are not exact because there is sometimes debate as to what constitutes a quotation, but they give a good impression of the distribution, some 93 per cent occurring in the letters to the Romans, Galatians and Corinthians (see also Appendix 2: Index of Paul's quotations).

It should be noted that this does not mean that letters like Philippians and Colossians show no interest in Scripture. Paul's statement that one day, 'at the name of Jesus every knee should bend, in heaven and on earth and under the earth, and every tongue should confess that Jesus Christ is Lord' (Phil. 2.10–12) is certainly drawing on Isaiah 45.23, where God says: 'To me every knee shall bow, every tongue shall swear.' Indeed, Paul quotes this text in Romans 14.11 (but applied to God rather than Christ), and we shall make reference to Philippians when we discuss it. But it does not constitute a quotation in Philippians and is better categorized as an allusion.

2

Letter	Scriptural references
Romans	60
1 Corinthians	17
2 Corinthians	10
Galatians	10
Ephesians	5
Philippians	0
1 Thessalonians	0
2 Thessalonians	0
1 Timothy	1
2 Timothy	1
Titus	0
Philemon	0

Paul – the early years

Before we embark on our study of Paul and Scripture we need to say something about Paul's background. From his own letters we learn that he was a Jew, of the tribe of Benjamin, and a member of the Pharisees (Phil. 3.5). He was proud of his heritage, believing that Israel had been entrusted with the 'oracles of God' (Rom. 3.2), which he elaborates as possessing the 'adoption, the glory, the covenants, the giving of the law, the worship, and the promises' (Rom. 9.4). His early life was characterized by 'zeal' for these traditions; indeed, he can speak of advancing in Judaism 'beyond many among my people of the same age, for I was far more zealous for the traditions of my ancestors' (Gal. 1.14). To the modern reader this might sound like a description of a conscientious religious person who studied a lot and prayed a lot. But 'zeal' has a more specific meaning in a first-century Jewish context. People like Phinehas (Num. 25) and Elijah (2 Kings 10) were remembered for their 'zeal' for God, which not only involved strict adherence to God's laws but violent opposition to those who broke them or caused others to break them. That Paul belonged to such a tradition is shown by his reaction to the early Church: 'I was violently persecuting the church of God and was trying to destroy it' (Gal. 1.13). It is probably also reflected in his condemnation of pagan behaviour in Romans 1.18–32, which ends: 'They know God's decree, that those who practise such things deserve to die – yet they not only do them but even applaud others who practise them.'

We also learn from Philippians 3.5 that Paul was a Pharisee – but what type of Pharisee? In the generation before Paul, two parties had become dominant among the Pharisees, led by Rabbi Hillel and Rabbi Shammai. Our knowledge of them comes mainly from the Mishnah, a collection of laws and rulings that were codified around 200 CE. In these rulings the strict opinion of Shammai is often contrasted with the more liberal opinion of Hillel. From Paul's statement in Philippians 3.6 ('as to righteousness under the law, blameless'), it would appear that he belonged to the strict party. Not only did he follow the general principle of the Pharisees that the written law, complemented by the oral law, could and should be lived out in daily life, he was also active in challenging anything that stood in the way of it. And since the Jews were under Roman rule this inevitably had political implications. Paul not only shared the hopes of his people that God would once again 'raise up the booth of David that is fallen' (Amos 9.11 – a text quoted in Acts and the Dead Sea Scrolls), he also believed that he had a role to play in preparing for it.

The author of Acts – traditionally thought to be Luke – tells us that Paul's Jewish name was Saul and that he came from a city called Tarsus in Cilicia (modern Turkey, just north of Cyprus). According to the historian Strabo, Tarsus was the home of a famous school or university that in certain respects surpassed even those at Athens and Alexandria. Its leading teachers were Stoics (Stoicism was a form of Greek philosophy) and it is possible that Greek and Latin literature formed part of Paul's education. Certainly his letters display a powerful rhetorical style, which makes it unlikely that he learnt Greek solely to converse with non-Jews. And as we shall see later, he is thoroughly at home in using the Greek translation of the Hebrew Scriptures known as the Septuagint, or LXX, from the legend that it was translated by 72 Jewish scholars in 72 days. In all likelihood he learnt Greek as a child, and although his letters would not be confused with classical literature, they have their own eloquence and fluency. Thus his 'zeal' does not appear to have been directed against 'all things Greek', though he may have shunned Greek philosophy.

Acts also tells us that he studied under Rabbi Gamaliel in Jerusalem, where he was 'educated strictly according to...ancestral law, being zealous for God' (Acts 22.3). This reference is slightly puzzling in that we know from other sources that Gamaliel represented the more lenient Hillel party. However, it is not uncommon for students to disagree with their teachers, and the reference to zeal might indicate that such tendencies were already present in the youthful Paul. On the other hand, some scholars think that Luke was mistaken, perhaps deducing that the great apostle 'must' have studied under the great rabbi. Where the two sources agree is that Paul was a persecutor of the Church. Acts 8.1 has just a cursory mention that Paul approved of the stoning of Stephen, but in Acts 9.1 we are told that 'Saul, still breathing threats and murder against the disciples of the Lord, went to the high priest and asked him for letters to the synagogues at Damascus, so that if he found any who belonged to the Way, men or women, he might bring them bound to Jerusalem'. It was on such a journey that Paul's life was turned upside down.

Paul's Damascus-road experience

Paul says very little about his 'conversion', or 'call', as some prefer to describe it. In Galatians 1.16, after stating that he used to be a persecutor of the Church, he says that God was pleased 'to reveal his Son to me, so that I might proclaim him among the Gentiles'. In the debates he is tackling in 1 Corinthians he finds it necessary to assert that he also has seen the Lord. In 1 Corinthians 9.1 this is posed as a rhetorical question: 'Have I not seen Jesus our Lord?' In 1 Corinthians 15.5–8 he is listing the witnesses to the resurrection (Peter, the Twelve, a crowd of over 500), and ends with this statement: 'Last of all, as to someone untimely born, he appeared also to me. For I am the least of the apostles, unfit to be called an apostle, because I persecuted the church of God.' These brief descriptions of this turning point in Paul's life are greatly amplified in Acts, where the experience and its aftermath are narrated on no fewer than three occasions (9.1–30; 22.1–21; 26.1–23). The shortest account puts it like this:

> I was travelling to Damascus with the authority and commission of the chief priests, when at midday along the road, your Excellency, I saw a light from heaven, brighter than the sun, shining around me and my companions. When we had all fallen to the ground, I heard a voice saying to me in the Hebrew language, 'Saul, Saul, why are you persecuting me? It hurts you to kick against the goads.' I asked, 'Who are you, Lord?' The Lord answered, 'I am Jesus whom you are persecuting. But get up and stand on your feet; for I have appeared to you for this purpose, to appoint you to serve and testify to the things in which you have seen me and to those in which I will appear to you.

> I will rescue you from your people and from the Gentiles – to whom I am sending you to open their eyes so that they may turn from darkness to light and from the power of Satan to God, so that they may receive forgiveness of sins and a place among those who are sanctified by faith in me.'

(Acts 26.12–18)

To what extent this represents an imaginative expansion of the tradition is not clear. What we can say is that it agrees with Paul's central claims: first, that he had a vision of Jesus; second, that it happened in the vicinity of Damascus; third, that it resulted in a vocation to preach the gospel to the Gentiles. Krister Stendahl (1976) famously questioned the use of the term 'conversion' to describe this since Paul was not changing from one religion (Judaism) to another (Christianity).[1] Even some 20 years after the event, Paul could cite himself as proof that God has not rejected his people, since 'I myself am an Israelite, a descendant of Abraham, a member of the tribe of Benjamin' (Rom. 11.1). Stendahl suggested that Paul received a new vocation or calling but not a conversion. However, while most scholars acknowledge the point, most people would recognize the upheaval in his thinking and change of direction in his life as conversion.

Paul – missionary, pastor and theologian

Reconstructing 'what happened next' is not easy. From Galatians 1.17 we learn that Paul immediately went to Arabia and afterwards to Damascus, either for reflection (the older view) or missionary work (the newer view). Three years later, he paid a brief visit to Jerusalem (Gal. 1.18–19) and then worked in the regions of Syria (based in Antioch) and Cilicia (where his home town is located). Some 14 years later – it is unclear if this includes the three years or not – he went up to Jerusalem to settle a dispute that was threatening the viability of his Gentile mission, namely whether Gentile converts needed to be circumcised and taught to obey the Jewish law (Gal. 2.1–10). From Paul's point of view the outcome was successful, and 'even Titus, who was with me, was not compelled to be circumcised, though he was a Greek' (Gal. 2.3). However, Paul then goes on to narrate a falling out with Peter at Antioch. Up until 'certain people came from James' (Gal. 2.12), Peter was happy to eat with the Gentiles, but when they

6

arrived, he withdrew and only ate with his fellow Jews. Paul was livid, not only accusing Peter of hypocrisy but also of undermining the gospel. As we shall see in subsequent chapters, this dispute had important repercussions for Paul's thinking about the significance of Abraham, Moses and the law.

Acts agrees that Paul spent some time in Damascus and Antioch, and adds the interesting detail that it was Barnabas who went to Tarsus (in Cilicia) to find Paul and bring him back to Antioch, where they worked for a year (11.25–26). It then gives a detailed account of missionary work in Cilicia and beyond (via a sea journey to Cyprus), before describing the celebrated Jerusalem council in chapter 15. This sequence fits quite well with what Paul tells us, except for the following. First, Acts 9.26–30 says that Paul left Damascus and came to Jerusalem, where he engaged in missionary work among the Jews. In Galatians, Paul seems adamant that he did not spend any length of time in Jerusalem. Second, Acts 15 resulted in a decree that accepted that Gentiles do not need to be circumcised but added that they should 'abstain from what has been sacrificed to idols and from blood and from what is strangled and from fornication' (Acts 15.29). In Galatians, Paul appears to claim that no conditions were imposed, though it is possible that he might not have regarded these as conditions. Third, Acts makes no mention of a falling out with Peter though, interestingly, it does describe a falling out with Barnabas (Acts 15.39).

What is clear from both Paul and Acts is that around 49 or 50 CE the Church came very close to schism over the issue of whether Gentiles needed to be circumcised and obey the law. This might seem a relatively trivial issue to us, but for them it concerned the authority of God's law, for Genesis 17 could hardly be clearer:

> As for you, you shall keep my covenant, you and your offspring after you throughout their generations. This is my covenant, which you shall keep, between me and you and your offspring after you: Every male among you shall be circumcised. You shall circumcise the flesh of your foreskins, and it shall be a sign of the covenant between me and you. Throughout your generations every male among you shall be circumcised when he is eight days old, including the slave born in your house and the one bought with your money from any foreigner who is not of your offspring.
>
> (Gen. 17.9–12)

Furthermore, Jesus was circumcised, and nowhere in the Gospels do we find a saying suggesting that this is no longer in force. Indeed, Matthew has Jesus declaring that 'whoever breaks one of the least of these commandments, and teaches others to do the same, will be called least in the kingdom of heaven' (Matt. 5.19). How then can Paul claim that he upholds the law (Rom. 3.31), while warning the Galatians that 'if you let yourselves be circumcised, Christ will be of no benefit to you' (Gal. 5.2)? We shall explore this in Chapters 2 and 3 but for now shall simply note that Paul's arguments did not necessarily convince everyone. In Acts 21 we are told that Paul returns to Jerusalem after preaching in Greece and Macedonia and tells James and the elders about all that 'God had done among the Gentiles through his ministry' (v. 19). This is initially welcomed ('When they heard it, they praised God', v. 20), but what follows somewhat undercuts it, for James says to Paul: 'You see, brother, how many thousands of believers there are among the Jews, and they are all zealous for the law. They have been told about you that you teach all the Jews living among the Gentiles to forsake Moses, and that you tell them not to circumcise their children or observe the customs' (vv. 20–21). James has a solution to persuade the Jewish believers that this is not true. He urges Paul to join a group of men who have taken a vow and thus demonstrate 'that you yourself observe and guard the law' (v. 24). James then reminds Paul of the decree that was sent to the Gentiles, but only refers to the prohibitions: 'But as for the Gentiles who have become believers, we have sent a letter with our judgement that they should abstain from what has been sacrificed to idols and from blood and from what is strangled and from fornication' (v. 25). Thus the reader of Galatians and Romans is likely to conclude that Paul's arguments won the day, whereas Acts suggests they had little impact on the Christians of Judea.

Paul and Scripture

As noted above, Paul is thoroughly at home with the Greek translation of the Scriptures known as the Septuagint (LXX). However, we need to say a little more about what Paul would have regarded as Scripture and what sort of texts were known to him. The Hebrew Bible that has come down to us – known as the Masoretic Text, or MT – is divided into three sections: law, prophets and writings. There is little doubt that the first five books – Torah in Hebrew; Pentateuch in Greek – that make up the first section were foundational for all forms of Judaism. Indeed, one of the reasons the Sadducees did not accept the doctrine of resurrection was that it cannot be demonstrated from the Torah (hence the significance of Jesus' reply in Mark 12.18–27). The second section is divided into the former prophets – what Christians would call the historical books from Joshua to 2 Kings – and the latter prophets (Isaiah, Jeremiah, Ezekiel and the Twelve). This was also relatively fixed, though texts found at Qumran show that there were variations in both wording and order. The third section (writings) consists of the psalms, wisdom books (Proverbs, Job, Song of Songs, Ecclesiastes), along with Ruth, Lamentations, Esther, Daniel, Ezra, Nehemiah and Chronicles. There is much more debate as to whether this was regarded as a fixed collection in Paul's day. Luke can end his Gospel by having Jesus say: 'everything written about me in the law of Moses, the prophets, and the psalms must be fulfilled' (Luke 24.44). This could be referring to the three-fold division (psalms standing for writings) or it may indicate a certain fluidity about what was included in the writings at this point in time.

Of greater significance for our study is that despite the legend that 72 Jewish scholars miraculously agreed in their translations of the Hebrew Scriptures, it is clear that it was in fact translated in stages. Thus the Pentateuch translation tends to be fairly literal and frequently preserves the word order of the Hebrew (even though the languages have quite different structures). It was almost certainly the first section to be translated. Other books are translated with more freedom and indeed, in some cases, incorporate verses and even whole chapters not present in the corresponding Hebrew book. The book of Daniel, for example, has an additional 67 verses between the Hebrew text of Daniel 3.23 and 3.24, which provide an explanation for why the three young men were unharmed by the fiery furnace: 'But the angel of the Lord came down into the furnace...and drove the fiery flame out of the furnace, and made the inside of the furnace as though a moist wind were whistling through it.' It also offers a long prayer by a certain Azaraiah, who joined them in the furnace, and a song of praise by the three men. When the Bible was translated into Latin (Vulgate, fifth century), this additional material was included and can be found in modern Roman Catholic Bibles, such as the Jerusalem Bible (JB). However, at the Reformation this material was classed as 'deutero-canonical', or 'apocryphal', and was not included in the King James Version (KJV) or its subsequent revisions.

There are also a number of additional books in the LXX that are not in the Hebrew Bible, such as Tobit, Judith, 1—4 Maccabees, Sirach and the Psalms of Solomon. Most of these are printed in the New Jerusalem Bible (NJB) but the New Revised Standard Version (NRSV) prints them separately under the heading of Apocrypha. The Protestant Bible only includes those books that are present in the Hebrew Bible, though interestingly prints them in the LXX order (e.g. Ruth, Ezra, Nehemiah and Chronicles are now among the historical books, while Daniel is with the prophets). There does not appear to be any explicit quotation of these 'deutero-canonical' books in Paul's undisputed letters, but he does appear to allude to some of them on occasion. One of the most difficult aspects of our study is to try to imagine what quoting or alluding to Scripture would have meant for someone like Paul. He would not have had our concept of 'Bible', a bound volume of 66 books (for Protestants) residing on his bookshelf. If the tradition about Gamaliel is correct, he would have known the Hebrew scrolls in use in Jerusalem and perhaps the LXX scrolls from Tarsus. His habit of preaching in the synagogues (Acts 13.14) would have alerted him to the fact that these scrolls sometimes differed, and would have brought familiarity with the Aramaic paraphrases known as Targumim (singular Targum), which increasingly accompanied readings of Scripture since many Jews could no longer understand Hebrew. So when Paul introduces a phrase or sentence with an introductory formula (IF) such as 'as it is written', we have to ask ourselves which version of the Scriptures he has in mind.

Introductory formulae (IF)

Quotations are often divided into *marked* and *unmarked*. Marked quotations are introduced by an introductory formula (IF), which might be elaborate, as in Matthew 1.22 ('All this took place to fulfil what had been spoken by the Lord through the prophet'), simple, as in Romans 1.17 ('as it is written') or a single word like 'for' (Rom. 10.13) or 'but' (Rom. 9.7). Unmarked quotations are woven into the author's prose but are identified by close verbal parallels to another text. Two questions arise from this: Is there a rationale for why some quotations are marked and others are not? Does the IF tell us anything about the author's attitude to the particular text and why it is being quoted?

Paul's introductory formulae can therefore be divided into those that use a verb of writing (generally 'as it is written') and those that use a verb of speaking (a whole variety of expressions, such as 'scripture says', 'he says', 'Isaiah/David/Moses/Hosea says', 'the law says', 'righteousness of faith says', 'God said', 'Isaiah cries out'). Is there a difference of attitude in using 'Moses says' and 'God says'? Or is naming the human author simply an aid to finding the passage? These questions continue to be debated.

A modern example illustrates the difficulty. If I am listening to a sermon and the preacher quotes Paul as saying, 'He who through faith is righteous shall live', I will recognize this as a quotation of Romans 1.17. However, I am familiar with this text from the NRSV, which says, 'The one who is righteous will live by faith.' It agrees that the righteous live by faith but does not say anything about *how* they obtained this righteousness. I might conclude, therefore, that the preacher has deliberately changed the wording of Romans 1.17 in order to ensure that the congregation adhere to the Reformation principle that righteousness comes through faith alone. However, there are two other options: first, the preacher might simply be quoting from the earlier Revised Standard Version (RSV), which says 'He who through faith is righteous shall live'; second, the preacher might have decided to quote from the RSV on this occasion because it offers better support for the point he or she wishes to make.

Similarly, when Paul brings his condemnation of hypocritical Jewish teachers to a close in Romans 2.24, he says: 'For, as it is written, "The name of God is blasphemed among the Gentiles because of you."' Now most scholars believe that this is a quotation from Isaiah 52.5, but the Hebrew Masoretic Text lacks the key phrases 'among the Gentiles' and 'because of you'. The Hebrew text simply says, 'and continually, all day long, my name is despised', which neither blames the Jews nor mentions the Gentiles, and thus hardly supports Paul's argument. Now it is possible that Paul is quoting a Hebrew text that he knows but that has not survived, and there are some examples where scholars think this might be the most plausible solution. However, in this case the explanation would appear to be that Paul is quoting the LXX of Isaiah 52.5, which reads: 'because of you, continually, my name is blasphemed among the Gentiles'. It still differs from Paul's precise words (he substitutes 'name of God' for 'my name'), and there is a change of word order; but most scholars think that these are Paul's modifications rather than his use of a different text.

In this book I will generally quote the Bible from the NRSV (Anglicized edition) as it is readily available, but when I need to demonstrate particular agreements or disagreements I provide my own translation and use the abbreviation 'lit.' (literally) and adhere closely to the original word order – even though it will result in some poor English. Thus I will indicate the agreements and disagreements between Paul's quotation in Romans 1.17 and the Hebrew and LXX of Habakkuk 2.4 as follows:

Hebrew text:	lit. 'but the righteous by his faithfulness will live'
LXX text:	lit. 'but the righteous by my faithfulness will live'
Paul's quotation:	lit. 'but the righteous by faith will live'

It is of interest that Habakkuk 2.4 is also quoted in Hebrews 10.38 and is probably to be rendered: lit. 'but my righteous by faith will live'. It would therefore appear that Habakkuk 2.4 was known in the first century in a variety of forms ('his faithfulness', 'my faithfulness', 'my righteous'), and what is therefore of note in Paul's quotation is that it lacks either a first-person pronoun ('my') or a third-person pronoun ('his'). We will discuss the possible reasons for this in Chapter 4. It should also be noted that many scholars reject the expression 'Old Testament' since Paul would not have regarded the Scriptures as 'old' (there was no 'New Testament' at this point). This is an important point, but there are also difficulties with the main alternatives: 'first testament' suffers from the same problem (Paul would not have understood 'first'), and 'Hebrew Bible' is misleading, given that Paul generally quoted from a Greek version. We thus retain the term 'Old Testament' as a reference to a body of literature, mindful that for Paul it was not 'old'.

New English Translation of the Septuagint (NETS)

Since Paul is writing in Greek to a Greek-speaking audience, his quotations are generally from the LXX (or a version of it). There have only been two translations of the LXX into English, that of the American scholar Charles Thomson (1808) and the English cleric, Sir Lancelot Brenton (1844). But in 2007, a group of scholars used the latest manuscript evidence to produce NETS.[2] This is an extremely useful resource for two reasons. First, each book or section of the LXX is introduced by a short essay on the characteristics of the LXX translator. Second, it has adopted the strategy of conforming the translation to the NRSV whenever the Greek and Hebrew are close, and departing from it when they are not. The English reader can therefore compare the NRSV and NETS and get some impression of the similarities and differences between the Greek and Hebrew versions, and the effect of these on the meaning of the text. As an example, Appendix 1 lists Paul's quotations from Isaiah, and one can easily see that there are significant differences – indicated by italics – in the meaning of Isaiah 8.14; 10.22–23; 11.10; 25.8; 52.5 and 52.7.

Plan of the book

We begin our study with Paul's use of the creation accounts and, in particular, the figure of Adam. Like his contemporaries, Paul uses the Adam story as a way of understanding the human condition, but unlike them he draws a parallel between Adam and Christ. He develops this in 1 Corinthians 15 and Romans 5, though it might also lie behind some of his other arguments. We then turn (Chapter 2) to Paul's use of the Abraham stories, which are critical for his understanding of faith and the people of God. He also constructs a number of arguments from the tradition that Abraham had two sons, one from his wife Sarah (Isaac) and one from the maid Hagar (Ishmael). He uses these to show that God's promises are not necessarily constrained by physical descent.

In Chapter 3 we consider Paul's use of the Moses (and Sinai) traditions. He draws on the conflict between Moses and Pharaoh as an illustration of divine hardening, and finds in Israel's wilderness experiences many lessons for the Christian community. But ultimately, Paul labels Moses' work as a 'ministry of death' (2 Cor. 3.7), which he contrasts with his own ministry of life and Spirit. The fact that Paul can say both positive and negative things about the law leads to Chapter 4. As well as specific studies in Paul's use of Scripture, scholars have been engaged in a huge debate on 'Paul and the law'. The difficulty is that he can speak in glowing terms that the law is spiritual and good (Rom. 7.12) and that his ministry upholds it (Rom. 3.31), while also declaring that it belongs to the old age and Christians should have nothing to do with it (Gal. 4). Thus in Chapter 4 we review a number of solutions to this problem, including what has become known as the 'New Perspective on Paul', a complete rethink of the works/faith dichotomy that has characterized Protestant thought on the subject.

Next we consider Paul's use of the prophets, and as this is an extensive topic we divide it into two chapters. Chapter 5 looks at the way Paul uses the prophets to explain how it has always been God's purpose to include Gentiles, as well as to predict a period of unbelief for the Jews. Chapter 6 looks at the way Paul uses the prophets to regulate the life of the Christian community (e.g. in matters of spiritual discernment, speaking in tongues, purity and separation), as well as to support his understanding of resurrection (1 Cor. 15).

Paul's use of the third section of the Hebrew Bible (writings) is the subject of Chapter 7. Paul makes extensive use of the psalms, but seldom to express praise (only Romans 15). Instead, he uses them in much the same way he uses the prophets: proclamation of the gospel; inclusion of the Gentiles; current unbelief of the Jews; future salvation; his own vocation and particular issues in the Church (e.g. Christian giving, acceptance of suffering). He does not make much use of Proverbs and Job, but there are a few quotations and allusions.

Finally, in Chapter 8 we consider a number of modern approaches to the study of Paul's use of Scripture. We begin by dividing such approaches into three categories: intertextual, narrative and rhetorical. The first focuses on the surrounding context of the quoted text, suggesting that when it is quoted, it brings with it associations and connotations from its original context. The second focuses on the narrative framework to which the quoted text belongs. It suggests that the associations and connotations that a text brings with it are not so much from the surrounding context as from the larger story. The third focuses on how Paul uses the text to convince or persuade his readers to accept the point he is making. We conclude with a brief summary of some of the important studies that continue to inform the subject, and advice on further reading.

1

Paul and the creation stories

Introduction

It is hardly surprising that the creation and fall stories of Genesis 1—3 would be the subject of speculation. The stories raise many questions: What does it mean to be in the image of God (Gen. 1.27)? What is the nature of humanity (Gen. 2.7)? What are the consequences of Adam's disobedience (Gen. 3.14–19)? Is it possible to return to the garden of Eden or is humanity forever doomed (Gen. 3.24)? Writers such as Philo of Alexandria, a Jewish philosopher contemporary with Paul, and books such as Wisdom of Solomon (included in the LXX) attempt to explore these questions. Philo, for example, draws on the different emphases of Genesis 1 (God creates by the utterance of a word) and Genesis 2 (God creates by forming from the dust) to distinguish between those who live by reason or philosophy and those who live by pleasure and sensual experience: 'The latter is a moulded clod of earth, the other is the faithful impress of the divine image.'[1] In Wisdom of Solomon an explanation is offered for humanity's subsequent degradation. Human beings should have recognized the invisible God from the 'greatness and beauty of created things' (Wisd. 13.5). This failure to discern God from the 'good things that are seen' was humanity's 'foolishness' (Wisd. 13.1) and led to idolatry, the worship of things created rather than the creator. Idolatry was not present in the beginning but when it was practised, it inevitably led to immorality (Wisd. 13.12–13). Though the relationship between the Wisdom of Solomon and Paul is debated, it is clear that Paul knows of such traditions when he writes of humanity's descent into sin in Romans 1 – see Table 1.1 overleaf.

Table 1.1

Wisdom of Solomon	Romans
For from the greatness and beauty of created things comes a corresponding perception of their Creator. (13.5)	Ever since the creation of the world his eternal power and divine nature, invisible though they are, have been understood and seen through the things he has made.
For all people who were ignorant of God were foolish by nature; and they were unable from the good things that are seen to know the one who exists. (13.1)	So they are without excuse; for though they knew God, they did not honour him as God or give thanks to him, but they became futile in their thinking, and their senseless minds were darkened.
But miserable, with their hopes set on dead things, are those who give the name 'gods' to the works of human hands, gold and silver fashioned with skill, and likenesses of animals, or a useless stone, the work of an ancient hand. (13.10)	Claiming to be wise, they became fools; and they exchanged the glory of the immortal God for images resembling a mortal human being or birds or four-footed animals or reptiles. (1.20–23)
For the idea of making idols was the beginning of fornication, and the invention of them was the corruption of life; for they did not exist from the beginning, nor will they last for ever. (14.12–13)	And since they did not see fit to acknowledge God, God gave them up to a debased mind and to things that should not be done. They were filled with every kind of wickedness, evil, covetousness, malice. (1.28–29)

Creation

Paul inherits from his Jewish tradition that the 'earth and all its fullness are the Lord's' (1 Cor. 10.26, quoting Ps. 24.1), despite the fact that things have gone dreadfully wrong. His only quotation from the creation stories comes in 2 Corinthians 4.6, where he wishes to assert that it is the same God who said 'Let light shine out of darkness' (Gen. 1.3) who has 'shone in our hearts to give the light of the knowledge of the glory of God in the face of Jesus Christ'. This could have a polemical edge against a group, later known as Gnostics, who maintained that the material world was the product of an inferior God and not the spiritual Father of Jesus Christ. Though Paul does make use of a flesh/spirit dichotomy in 1 Corinthians 15, it is not at the expense of denying that creation was good. The saviour is not undoing the work of an inferior creator.

The most detailed use of the creation stories comes in 1 Corinthians 15. It would appear that some – perhaps the same group as above – were ridiculing the idea of a bodily resurrection in favour of a purely spiritual existence in the afterlife: 'But someone will ask, "How are the dead raised? With what kind of body do they come?"' (1 Cor. 15.35). This would have been a common objection from those influenced by Greek thought, where the 'soul' was either thought to live on after death (immortality) or go through a series of rebirths. The idea that this 'soul' requires another 'body' in the afterlife would not only have seemed strange to a Greek audience but also rather unsophisticated. Can Paul not rise above such 'material' thought and envisage a purely 'spiritual' existence?

It should also be noted that the idea of resurrection was a matter of dispute within contemporary Judaism. The Pharisees were broadly in favour of it but the Sadducees maintained that it was a recent innovation and could not be demonstrated from the law (Pentateuch). In fact clear references to resurrection in the Old Testament are limited to a few texts, of which Daniel 12.1–2 is the most explicit: 'Many of those who sleep in the dust of the earth shall awake, some to everlasting life, and some to shame and everlasting contempt' (v. 2). This text says nothing about the *form* of this post-mortem existence but the metaphor of 'awaking' is suggestive of some sort of resurrection rather than immortality.

Paul begins his defence of 'bodily' resurrection by pointing out that God has given different types of flesh (*sarx*) to the different animals: 'Not all flesh is alike, but there is one flesh for human beings, another for animals, another for birds, and another for fish' (1 Cor. 15.39). That Paul has the creation account in mind is confirmed by 1 Corinthians 15.41, where he refers to the different heavenly bodies: 'There is one glory of the sun, and another glory of the moon, and another glory of the stars; indeed, star differs from star in glory.' Paul's point is that since God gave an appropriate 'flesh' to animals, fish and birds so that they could flourish in their respective environments, the same will be true of the afterlife: 'So it is with the resurrection of the dead.' This is not a materialistic concept of the afterlife, for Paul calls it a 'spiritual body' (*soma pneumatikos*), which he distinguishes from an ordinary 'physical body' (*soma psychikos*). Paul does not speculate on the nature of this 'spiritual body', nor does he seek to answer the question that many people ask at funerals: 'Will I recognize my loved one in the afterlife?' But it is clear from other statements that he believes that this 'spiritual body' will resemble the resurrection body of Christ: 'He will transform the body of our humiliation [*or* humble body] that it may be conformed to the body of his glory [*or* glorious body]' (Phil. 3.21).

Just as the cosmic creation of Genesis 1 is followed by the particular description of Adam and Eve in Genesis 2, so Paul moves on to describe Adam as 'from the earth, a man of dust' in 1 Corinthians 15.47. Before we examine his argument, it is necessary to say something about the word 'Adam'. The Hebrew word *adam* first occurs in Genesis 1.26–27, where God says: 'Let us make *adam* in our image…male and female he created them.' The reference to 'male and female' suggests that the meaning is generic, and the NRSV renders it 'humankind', in preference to 'man' or 'mankind'. The next occurrence is in Genesis 2.5, where it is said that there was no *ha-adam* to till the earth (*adamah*). The connection between the two words is made clearer in the following verse, where God 'forms' *ha-adam* from the earth (*adamah*). The prefix *ha-* represents the definite article and occurs with *adam* on more than 500 occasions in the Hebrew Bible. Grammatically, it could be singular ('the man'), generic ('humankind') or a proper noun ('Adam'). The NRSV renders Genesis 2.7: 'then the LORD God formed *man* from the dust of the ground, and breathed into his nostrils the breath of life; and *the man* became a living being'.

In Genesis 2.8 the 'earth-man' is placed in the garden of Eden, which is repeated in Genesis 2.15. In all of these references the LXX uses *anthropos* ('man, person') but in Genesis 2.16 it changes to the proper name Adam (lit. 'and the LORD God commanded Adam') but returns to *anthropos* in Genesis 2.18 (lit. 'It is not good that the man is alone'). Thereafter it uses Adam, and the KJV follows suit. However, more recent translations have delayed speaking of Adam until 2.20 (NIV), 3.17 (RSV) and 4.25 (NRSV, NJB) – see Table 1.2 opposite.

Returning to Paul, Adam was more than just a 'man of dust', for God 'breathed into his nostrils the breath of life; and the man became a living being' (Gen. 2.7). Paul quotes this text while adding a statement about Jesus, who he calls 'the last Adam'. A reader who was

Table 1.2

Genesis	KJV	NIV	RSV	NRSV
1.26 let us make *adam* in our image	man	man	man	humankind
1.27 and so God made *ha-adam*	man	man	man	humankind
2.5 there was no *ha-adam* to till the earth	man	man	man	one
2.7 then the Lord God formed *ha-adam*	man	the man	man	the man
2.8 and there he put *ha-adam*	the man	the man	the man	the man
2.15 the Lord God took *ha-adam*	the man	the man	the man	the man
2.16 the Lord God commanded *ha-adam*	the man	the man	the man	the man
2.18 it is not good that *ha-adam* be alone	the man	the man	the man	the man
2.19 and brought them to *ha-adam*	Adam	the man	the man	the man
2.20 and *ha-adam* gave names	Adam	Adam	the man	the man
2.21 the Lord God caused *ha-adam* to sleep	Adam	the man	the man	the man
2.22 had taken from *ha-adam*	the man	the man	the man	the man
2.23 for out of *ha-adam*	Adam	the man	the man	the man
2.25 *ha-adam* and his wife	the man	the man	the man	the man
3.8 *ha-adam* and his wife	Adam	the man	the man	the man
3.9 the Lord God called *ha-adam*	Adam	the man	the man	the man
3.12 and *ha-adam* said	Adam	the man	the man	the man
3.17 and to *ha-adam* he said	Adam	Adam	Adam	the man
3.20 *ha-adam* named his wife Eve	Adam	Adam	the man	the man
3.21 the Lord God made *ha-adam*	Adam	Adam	Adam	the man
3.22 *ha-adam* has now become like one of us	the man	the man	the man	the man
3.24 he drove *ha-adam* out	the man	the man	the man	the man
4.1 *ha-adam* knew his wife Eve	Adam	Adam	Adam	the man
4.25 *ha-adam* knew his wife again	Adam	Adam	Adam	Adam

unaware of the Genesis text might assume that Scripture actually spoke about this 'last Adam', for Paul does not distinguish between his own words and the words of the quotation. The NRSV clarifies this by placing quotation marks around the first part only, but it should be noted that the original Greek manuscripts contained almost no punctuation – not even spaces between words. However, it is fairly certain that Paul's readers would recognize such a well-known text from the creation stories and deduce that the latter phrase is Paul's own comment: 'Thus it is written, "The first man, Adam, became a living being"; *the last Adam became a life-giving spirit*' (1 Cor. 15.45).

It is unclear what led Paul to describe Christ as the 'last Adam'. As he is clearly not the last person to be born, 'last' must have a more technical meaning. In what follows he calls Adam the first man and Christ the second man, suggesting that 'first' and 'last' refer to two great acts of God. Adam was from the dust and Christ was/is from heaven. From them come two types of people: those who are 'of the dust' and those who are 'of heaven' (1 Cor. 15.48). Now this sounds dangerously close to the dualism of Gnosticism, but Paul adds a temporal aspect: 'Just as we have borne the image of the man of dust, we will also bear the image of the man of heaven' (1 Cor. 15.49). Thus it is not the dualistic notion that the world is divided into 'earthly' and 'heavenly' people and only the latter will be saved. All are born 'earthly' but it is possible to become 'heavenly'. Indeed, it is necessary to become 'heavenly' for 'flesh and blood cannot inherit the kingdom of God' (1 Cor. 15.50). Paul does not at this point say how this comes about but calls it a 'mystery' and uses the verb *allasso* to describe this 'change': 'We will not all die, but we will all be changed.' The verb is not a technical term but can refer to a change of custom (Acts 6.14), a change of voice (Gal. 4.20) or a change of worship (Rom. 1.23).

Tom Wright offers an interesting rationale for Paul's use of the Adam–Christ typology. He notes that after Genesis 12, the original commission to be 'fruitful and multiply' and 'have dominion' is transferred to Abraham and his descendants (Gen. 12.2f.; 17.2f.; 22.16ff. etc.). Wright deduces from this and a range of Jewish references (e.g. *Jub.* 2.23; *1 Enoch* 90; *4 Ezra* 3) that Israel was thought to embody the purposes of humanity. But since Israel failed in this task, it fell to Christ, as Israel's representative, to accomplish them on her behalf.

As we shall see later, this is Wright's explanation of Galatians 3, where Christ absorbed the curse that had come upon Israel for her disobedience. According to Wright, therefore, the rationale for the Adam–Christ typology is that Jewish tradition had already associated Israel with Adam, and Christian tradition had already associated Christ with Israel. As far as we know, it was Paul's innovation to connect Adam with Christ.[2]

Earlier in the letter, Paul offers advice concerning orderly worship. First Corinthians 11.17–34 concerns the nature of the shared meal and the fact that the poor are being humiliated. Before that, Paul deals with the problem of women worshipping and praying without a suitable head covering. To a modern audience this seems a trivial issue, but in the culture of the time this was causing offence, at least to some. Paul argues on two grounds: nature and Scripture. For the first, he thinks that nature 'teaches' that women should have long hair, for 'it is disgraceful for a woman to have her hair cut off or to be shaved' (1 Cor. 11.6). This long hair is the woman's glory and acts as a 'covering'. Paul deduces from this that God wishes women to be 'covered' or 'veiled' when they worship, for 'any woman who prays or prophesies with her head unveiled disgraces her head – it is one and the same thing as having her head shaved' (1 Cor. 11.5). To us, this seems a rather arbitrary deduction to make. The opposite conclusion, that women do not need to cover their heads in worship because their long hair already provides such a covering, seems just as logical.

The scriptural argument is interesting because Paul makes certain moves towards a more inclusive position. He first notes that 'a man ought not to have his head veiled, since he is the image and reflection of God; but woman is the reflection of man' (1 Cor. 11.7). That Paul has the creation of Eve in mind is clear from what follows: 'Indeed, man was not made from woman, but woman from man. Neither was man created for the sake of woman, but woman for the sake of man' (1 Cor. 11.8–9). For Paul, the creation of Adam was direct and he bears the image and reflection of God. The creation of Eve was indirect and, according to Genesis 2.21–23, derives from 'Adam's rib'. This allows Paul to deduce that women should have an *exousia* on their head. The meaning of *exousia* is 'authority' or 'power', but is Paul referring to *her* authority (to pray and prophesy) or her need to be *under* authority (i.e. a man) in order to perform these functions? The

KJV rendered *exousia* with 'power' and could point to the first option: 'For this cause ought the woman to have power on her head.' Revisions such as the RSV, NRSV and NIV prefer to leave it ambiguous (as the Greek is), while the Jerusalem Bible prefers the second option, 'a symbol of authority *over them*'. The verse ends with an explanation that this is 'because of the angels', a statement that has thoroughly perplexed commentators all down the centuries.

Paul continues with a 'nevertheless' and notes that while it can be said that the woman came from the man in the first generation, all subsequent men have come from women. Thus there is a certain reciprocity between the sexes, for 'in the Lord woman is not independent of man or man independent of woman'. We see this same tendency in Paul's discussion of the marriage relationship in 1 Corinthians 7. When he states that 'the wife does not have authority over her own body, but the husband does', it sounds like Paul is about to repeat the patriarchal attitudes of his culture. But then he adds: 'likewise the husband does not have authority over his own body, but the wife does'. This breaking down of some of society's divisions is famously expressed in Galatians 3.28: 'There is no longer Jew or Greek, there is no longer slave or free, there is no longer male and female; for all of you are one in Christ Jesus.' It is possible that Paul is simply naming some of the most characteristic causes of tension in his culture and claiming that they are healed – or should be – in Christ. But the phrase 'male and female' would certainly suggest the creation stories, and it may be that Paul is thinking of Genesis 1.27, where we find a more inclusive vision than in the Adam and Eve story that follows: 'So God created humankind in his image, in the image of God he created them; male and female he created them.'

The fall

As it now stands, the description of the fall of Adam and Eve in Genesis 3 provides the explanation for what we would call today the human condition. That act of disobedience is the origin of fear (Gen. 3.10), pain (Gen. 3.16), struggle (Gen. 3.17) and death (Gen. 3.19; cf. Gen. 2.17). It is therefore surprising that the Old Testament hardly ever makes reference to the story, and when it does it is either ambiguous (Job 31.33 could be translated: 'If I conceal my transgression like Adam' or 'If I conceal my transgression like humanity does'; see also Hos. 6.7) or inconsequential (Deuteronomy 4.32:

'For ask now about former ages, long before your own, ever since the day that God created human beings on the earth'). Perhaps the most interesting reference is Ezekiel's condemnation of the king of Tyre, which clearly echoes 'the fall' story but is not being used to describe the human condition:

> You were in Eden, the garden of God; every precious stone was your covering...On the day that you were created they were prepared. With an anointed cherub as guardian I placed you; you were on the holy mountain of God; you walked among the stones of fire. You were blameless in your ways from the day that you were created, until iniquity was found in you.
>
> (Ezek. 28.13–15)

Of course, the Old Testament is under no illusions about human sinfulness. The beginning of the flood story starts with the words: 'The Lord saw that the wickedness of humankind was great in the earth, and that every inclination of the thoughts of their hearts was only evil continually' (Gen. 6.5). The psalmist declares that humanity has 'all gone astray, they are all alike perverse; there is no one who does good, no, not one' (Ps. 14.3). And Ecclesiastes 7.20 realizes that even the most righteous acts are tainted with sin: 'there is no one on earth so righteous as to do good without ever sinning'. Indeed, Paul can quote these texts, along with some colourful phrases from other psalms, to support the view that all people, both Jews and Greeks, are under the power of sin:

> There is no one who is righteous, not even one [Eccles. 7.20]; there is no one who has understanding, there is no one who seeks God. All have turned aside, together they have become worthless; there is no one who shows kindness, there is not even one [Ps. 14.1–3]. Their throats are opened graves; they use their tongues to deceive [Ps. 5.9]. The venom of vipers is under their lips [Ps. 140.3]. Their mouths are full of cursing and bitterness [Ps. 10.7]. Their feet are swift to shed blood; ruin and misery are in their paths, and the way of peace they have not known [Isa. 59.7–8]. There is no fear of God before their eyes [Ps. 36.1].
>
> (Rom. 3.10–18)

None of these Old Testament references connect this evil inclination with the fall of Adam and Eve, but this is precisely what Paul does in Romans 5.12–21. Texts like the Wisdom of Solomon offer Paul a precedent for finding the origin of human sinfulness in idolatry, the turning from worship of the creator to that which is created. Indeed, Wisdom goes further and stresses that death is not God's responsibility, 'because God did not make death, and he does not delight in the death of the living' (Wisd. 1.13). Human sinfulness is responsible for death because the 'ungodly by their words and deeds summoned death' (Wisd. 1.16). Paul agrees that the 'wages of sin is death' (Rom. 6.23) but traces the origin of death back to the original sin of Adam: 'death exercised dominion from Adam to Moses, even over those whose sins were not like the transgression of Adam' (Rom. 5.14). As in 1 Corinthians 15, Paul's discussion of Adam runs in parallel with his discussion of Christ, and it is intriguing to ask how the description of one has affected the description of the other. In other words, to what extent has Paul's understanding of the human condition affected his description of Christ as its saviour? And to what extent has his understanding of Christ as saviour affected his understanding of the human condition? This is a live debate in Pauline scholarship and is sometimes posed in this form: Did Paul's thought move primarily from 'plight to solution' or 'solution to plight'?

In order to begin to answer this, let us first summarize what Paul says about Adam and his sin in Romans 5.12–21. We have noted that it was through Adam that sin came into the world and sin brought death. Death spread to all because all sinned, even though their sin was not necessarily like the 'transgression' of Adam. Having stated this universal conclusion, Paul strangely talks about the effects of Adam's sin on 'the many'. Thus 'the many died through the one man's trespass'. This means more than the fact that at a given point of time they cease to exist, for judgement (*krima*) followed the one man's trespass, leading to condemnation (*katakrima*). Paul returns to a universal statement in 5.18 ('just as one man's trespass led to condemnation for all') but speaks of 'the many' in 5.19 ('by the one man's disobedience the many were made sinners'). This variation is puzzling, for while it might be possible to reconcile the latter pair (many are sinners but condemnation comes to all), the former pair (death comes to all, death comes to the many) cannot be reconciled. We can only conclude that it is stylistic variation and that the two terms mean the same thing.

Paul says in Romans 5.14 that Adam was a 'type' of the one to come. The word derives from the verb *typto*, which means 'to strike', and so is used of the 'mark' or 'impression' left by a die, or more generally, of a pattern or example. Thus Paul urges the Romans to follow the '*form* of teaching to which you have been entrusted' (Rom. 6.17) and in Philippians 3.17, to emulate his *pattern* or *example* of life (cf. 1 Thess. 1.7). Each of these examples are positive, but in 1 Corinthians 10.6 Paul urges his readers *not* to follow the example of those Israelites who rebelled against Moses in the desert. The word gives rise to the term 'typology', which in mathematics refers to the study of patterns and shapes but in Christian theology to the relationship between certain people, places or events in the New Testament and people, places or events in the Old Testament, which are thought to 'prefigure' them. An example from the Gospels is the saying about Jonah: 'For just as Jonah was three days and three nights in the belly of the sea monster, so for three days and three nights the Son of Man will be in the heart of the earth' (Matt. 12.40). It should be noted that the typology is limited to this aspect of Jonah's story; it is not suggesting that Jonah's earlier cowardice is also true of the 'Son of Man'.

Paul's typology of Adam and Christ is unusual in that he spends most of his time showing how they differ, both in their actions and the consequences that follow. He also oscillates between 'all' and 'many', as in his statements about Adam, hence the 'grace of God and the free gift in the grace of the one man, Jesus Christ, abounded for the many'. In contrast to judgement and condemnation, 'the free gift following many trespasses brings justification'. In contrast to death, 'much more surely will those who receive the abundance of grace and the free gift of righteousness exercise dominion in life through the one man, Jesus Christ'. The point of comparison between Adam and Christ is that one act has had universal effects. Adam is a 'type' of Christ in that his 'trespass led to condemnation for all', but Christ's 'act of righteousness (*dikaioma*) leads to justification and life (*dikaiosis zoes*) for all'. Paul's oscillation between 'all' and 'many' is not because he thinks that only a small group will be saved, for this last verse claims that Christ's 'act of righteousness' brings justification 'for all' (*eis pantas*). How he reconciles this with his belief that 'Fornicators, idolaters, adulterers, male prostitutes, sodomites, thieves, the greedy, drunkards, revilers, robbers' will not 'inherit the kingdom of God' (1 Cor. 6.9–10) is not clear. However, what we can say is that Romans 5 is not an isolated piece of wishful thinking. After the long discussion of God's plan for Israel and the rest of humanity in Romans 9—11, Paul concludes: 'For God has imprisoned all in disobedience so that he may be merciful *to all*' (Rom. 11.32). Paul's vision is universal in scope, though he recognizes that judgement is also a reality.

Original sin

In Romans 5.12, Paul says that death entered the world through Adam's sin and so death came to all because (*eph ho*) all sinned. It is now commonly agreed that the Greek words *eph ho* mean 'because' (Paul also uses them in 2 Corinthians 5.4 and Philippians 3.12, 4.10) and not 'in him' as Origen (c. 200 CE) took it and as it was translated into Latin (*in quo*). The Latin translation lends itself to an understanding of 'original sin' whereby death comes to all people because all people sinned 'in Adam'. The author of Hebrews offers an argument for the superiority of a priesthood of the order of Melchizedek by saying that when Abraham offered tithes to Melchizedek, Levi was involved in this act because he was 'still in the loins of Abraham' (Heb. 7.10). This shows that such an argument was possible in the first century, and why the Latin text could be taken to mean that all human beings are 'in Adam' and thus involved in his act of disobedience (and hence guilty). Whether such a doctrine can be constructed on other grounds is debated, but it is not what Paul is saying in Romans 5.12. Neither does he (nor any New Testament writing) ever suggest that Jesus had to be born of a virgin in order to break this connection with Adam's sin. Indeed, Paul's only mention of Christ's birth comes in Galatians 4.4–5, which stresses the similarity rather than dissimilarity with his contemporaries: 'But when the fullness of time had come, God sent his Son, born of a woman, born under the law, in order to redeem those who were under the law, so that we might receive adoption as children.'

There are two further passages that might have Adam in the background, though he is not mentioned by name. First, in Romans 7, Paul attempts to explain why human beings can aspire to that which is good but are constantly thwarted in accomplishing it. Paul writes in the first person, and scholars have debated whether he is talking about his pre-Christian life (from which he has now been saved) or his Christian life (the ongoing struggle between the promptings of the Spirit and the old self); a third view is that Paul is using the story of Adam to speak generally about the human condition, in which he himself is included. Thus Paul writes of a time when he was 'alive apart from the law' but 'sin, seizing an opportunity in the commandment, deceived me and through it killed me' (Rom. 7.9, 11). Coming soon after Romans 5, a reader is bound to see the parallel with Adam and deduce that Adam's experience is now reproduced in each one of us. As a result, Paul echoes the human (*adam*) condition when he says: 'when I want to do what is good, evil lies close at hand' (Rom. 7.21).

The second passage (Phil. 2.6–11) is more controversial, and the 'Adam' interpretation is particularly associated with James Dunn.[3] Most scholars have taken phrases like 'though he was in the form of God' and 'emptied himself, taking the form of a slave' as references to the incarnation. The 'form of God' is taken as a reference to divinity, whereas 'form of a slave' is taken as a reference to humanity. But seen in the light of the Adam tradition, Dunn suggests that it might have a more 'earthly' meaning. Paul's purpose in quoting the hymn is to give an example of humility rather than selfishness (Phil. 2.1–4). So in contrast to Adam, who was also in the form/image of God, Christ did not seek something higher but emptied himself, taking the form of a slave. The contrast is between the 'earthly' Adam wanting to be like God and the 'earthly' Jesus choosing to become a slave. This is the behaviour the quarrelling Philippians are being asked to emulate, not the decision of the divine Son of God to become human. However, having made this point, Dunn reminds us that we are dealing here with poetry and evocative allusion rather than doctrinal formulae, and perhaps the two interpretations are not mutually exclusive.

Creation's curse

In Romans 8, Paul states that the present sufferings are nothing compared with the glory that is to come. He then has a very interesting passage about creation 'groaning' in its state of decay, and 'looking forward' to its future redemption (Rom. 8.22, 19). This personification of the 'agonies' of creation has been the subject of intense study in the last 20 years, prompted by our mounting ecological crisis. The key verse is Romans 8.20, where he states that 'creation was subjected to futility, not of its own will but by the will of the one who subjected it, in hope'. Since the reference to the 'bondage of creation' is probably an allusion to Genesis 3.17 ('cursed is the ground because of you'), the identity of the 'one who subjected it' is most likely God, rather than Adam, humanity or the devil. But why has God subjected creation to futility? Paul's answer is so that it can participate in the redemption of humanity. God's purpose in salvation is not to 'remove' human beings from the earth and place them in heaven. Rather, it is nothing short of the redemption/restoration of the whole created order: 'the creation itself will be set free from its bondage to decay and will obtain the freedom of the glory of the children of God' (Rom. 8.21).

Paul's choice of the word 'futility' (*mataiotes*) would remind the knowledgeable reader of the book of Ecclesiastes, where it occurs 39 times in the LXX. The author – traditionally thought to be Solomon – observes the activities of humankind and declares them 'empty', 'vain' or 'futile'. The Hebrew word is *hebel*, rendered by *mataiotes* in the LXX. What is of particular interest for the interpretation of Romans 8 is that the first activity mentioned in Ecclesiastes is 'toil', which seems to make no ultimate difference to the earth. If this is also an allusion to Genesis 3.17 ('in toil you shall eat of it all the days of your life'), then it may be that Romans 8.20 can be explained as a combination of Genesis 3.17 and its later interpretation in Ecclesiastes 1. Because of Adam's transgression, life on earth is experienced as 'toil' (Gen. 3.17) and futility (Eccles. 1) but not without hope. One day, it will be part of God's redemption of the whole created order.

Let us now return to our question of whether Paul's thought primarily moves from 'plight to solution' or 'solution to plight'. As we saw at the beginning of the chapter, the Hebrew Bible has little to say about the fall, but it was the subject of speculation in other works, such as Wisdom of Solomon and a number of Philo's writings. Paul inherited the view of the first Christians that 'Christ died for our sins' (1 Cor. 15.3), but was it his understanding of the fall that led him to view this as fundamentally an act of obedience (i.e. 'plight to solution')? It is possible, but perhaps the opposite is more likely. Paul understood from his Damascus-road vision that Christ was

God's appointed agent of salvation. That being so, he deduced – or perhaps intuitively knew – that Christ is the solution to the 'human condition', including the curse pronounced in Genesis 3.17 on the earth. That is why he can say that the creation has been eagerly longing for the time when it will share in the 'glory of the children of God'. However, the advantage of 'solution to plight' for modern readers is that Paul's arguments might still have value now that the theory of evolution makes it impossible – for most people – to believe in a literal Adam and Eve. If Paul is making deductions about Christ and salvation based on the facticity of the Adam and Eve story, it is hard to see how they can continue to command support. But if Paul is using the Adam and Eve story to illustrate what he believed about Christ, then he has given us an interesting example of 'cultural communication'.

1 Timothy 2.11–15

One of the reasons why many scholars doubt that the Pastoral Epistles come directly from the hand of Paul is the treatment of the Adam and Eve story in 1 Timothy 2.11–15. As with 1 Corinthians 11, the argument depends on the second creation story (Gen. 2), where Adam is created first, followed by Eve. But 1 Timothy 2.14 then makes another point: 'Adam was not deceived, but the woman was deceived and became a transgressor.' The difficulty is not so much the statement that Eve was deceived, for Paul can say in 2 Corinthians 11.3 that 'the serpent deceived Eve by its cunning'; it is whether one can imagine the author of Romans 5, who declared that 'sin came into the world through one man', 'because of the one man's trespass, death exercised dominion' and 'one man's trespass led to condemnation for all' could possibly think that 'Adam was not deceived'. Advocates of Pauline authorship make the point that ten years had passed since the writing of Romans 5 and that it would be perfectly possible for Paul to use the Genesis passage to make a different point.

Conclusion

Although Paul echoes contemporary traditions concerning creation and fall (e.g. Wisdom of Solomon), it is clear that his interest is primarily christological. Thus his discussion of Adam in Romans 5 and 1 Corinthians 15 is really a discussion of Christ. Paul wants to assert that God is recreating humanity in Christ, and the story of Adam gives him a conceptual framework to do so, perhaps via Christ as Israel's representative. In 1 Corinthians 15, Paul is answering questions about the resurrection, and does so by contrasting the earthly existence of Adam with the heavenly existence of Christ. In other words, Paul believes certain things about Christ and uses the Genesis narratives to illustrate/support them.

However, from a literary perspective the linking of two things is bound to produce some mutual interpretation, and one can reasonably ask whether the Adam–Christ typology has had some effect on Paul's thinking about Christ. For example, he inherited the tradition that Christ's death was a sacrifice for sins (1 Cor. 15.3), but was it the Adam typology that prompted him to think of it as an act of obedience (Rom. 5.19)? The logic of the comparison leads Paul to assert that 'just as one man's trespass led to condemnation *for all*, so one man's act of righteousness leads to justification and life *for all*' (Rom. 5.18), which is in tension with many of his 'judgement' passages. This could be seen as evidence that the Adam–Christ typology has exerted some influence – though not the dominant influence – on Paul's thinking about Christ.

2

Paul and Abraham

Introduction

Abraham occupies a unique place in religious history. As well as being the forefather of the Jewish people he is also of great importance for Christianity and Islam. In the New Testament he is mentioned by name in each of the Gospels, Acts, Paul, Hebrews, James and 1 Peter, and Matthew begins his Gospel with the words: 'An account of the genealogy of Jesus the Messiah, the son of David, the son of Abraham' (Matt. 1.1). It is not surprising that the Abraham narratives found in Genesis 12—25 are arguably the most important texts for Paul. He mentions Abraham by name 17 times, concentrated in two expository sections (Gal. 3—4; Rom. 4). He also, in Romans 11.1 and 2 Corinthians 11.22, refers to himself as a descendant of Abraham. But Paul's exposition of Abraham did not take place in a vacuum. It competes with other interpretations that were being offered in the first century, sometimes agreeing and sometimes disagreeing. But before we consider this we will first offer a brief summary of the key events in Genesis 12—25.

Abraham in Genesis

Abraham is first introduced as Abram in Genesis 11.26, but it is the command to leave his homeland and travel to a foreign country in Genesis 12.1–3 that marks the beginning of his story. The command comes with a promise that Abraham will be a great nation and, even more staggering, that in Abraham, 'all the families of the earth shall be blessed' (Gen. 12.3). Abraham obeys, and the next few chapters see him caught up in various conflicts: with the Egyptian pharaoh; with his nephew Lot; with a confederation of kings. Genesis 15 marks the next stage in his relationship with God. It begins with Abraham questioning how he will be the father of a great nation when he is childless; indeed, at present, it is a slave born in his house who will be his heir. God responds that the slave will not be his heir, and shows him the stars of heaven, declaring, 'So shall your descendants be' (Gen. 15.5). God then makes a covenant with Abraham, involving a rather strange ritual of fire passing between the carcasses of a number of animals, confirming the promise that 'To your descendants I give this land' (Gen. 15.18).

The focus of the next section concerns the birth of the promised son. In some ancient cultures there was a custom that if a wife was unable to produce children, she should provide a surrogate so that the line would not die out. This is what Sarah does when she suggests that Abraham has sex with Hagar, her maid, and the result is the birth of Ishmael (Gen. 16). The text does not rebuke them for this action, but it is adamant that Ishmael is not the promised heir. Sarah will bear Abraham a son and he will be called Isaac (Gen. 17). Somewhat strangely, this chapter begins with God saying, 'I am God Almighty; walk before me, and be blameless. And I will make my covenant between me and you, and will make you exceedingly numerous' (Gen. 17.1–2). We are not told how this relates to the covenant of chapter 15, and stylistic differences between the chapters suggest that the author/editor has used different sources. Here, the focus is on circumcision as a sign of the covenant: 'This is my covenant, which you shall keep, between me and you and your offspring after you: Every male among you shall be circumcised' (Gen. 17.10).

Genesis 18—19 begins with the mysterious visit of the three messengers – captured in Andrei Rublev's famous icon – and narrates the story of the destruction of Sodom and Gomorrah and the rescue of Lot, Abraham's nephew. Genesis 20 is similar to an earlier story (12.10–20), where Abraham pretends that Sarah is his sister in order to avoid danger. In the light of the 'heroic' literature that followed it is noteworthy that the text is candid about Abraham's 'weakness', though it does not pass judgement on him.

Genesis 21 sees the birth of Isaac, exactly at the time God had promised. He was circumcised on the eighth day, as God had commanded, and the rest of the chapter concerns the rivalry between Sarah and Hagar. Sarah sees Ishmael 'playing' with Isaac and tells Abraham to send him and his mother away. This is displeasing to Abraham, but God assures him that he will not come to harm. Apart from this brief mention of Isaac (the story is about Ishmael), the first story about Isaac is when God 'tests' Abraham by commanding him to offer him as a sacrifice (Gen. 22.1). The text seems oblivious of the morality of such a command, but is well aware of its gravity: 'Take your son, *your only son* Isaac, *whom you love*, and go to the land of Moriah, and offer him there as a burnt offering' (Gen. 22.2). Not only is Abraham being asked to sacrifice his beloved son, this is also his only son, the promised heir. In the event, it is enough that Abraham shows willingness to obey God, and an angel intervenes before any harm is done (Gen. 22.12).

The stories of Abraham are brought to a conclusion by narrating the death and burial of Sarah (Gen. 23), the procurement of a wife (Rebecca) for Isaac (Gen. 24) and the death of Abraham at the age of 175 (Gen. 25). In this final chapter we are told that Abraham took another wife (Keturah) and had six further sons before being buried in the same cave as Sarah. The chapter details the sons of Ishmael before turning to its main focus: the birth of Jacob and Esau to Isaac and Rebecca.

Abraham in Jewish tradition

In the rest of the Old Testament, Abraham is generally mentioned as one of the three patriarchs (Abraham, Isaac and Jacob), and in phrases like 'the God of your ancestors, the God of Abraham, of Isaac and of Jacob' (Exod. 3.16; 1 Kings 18.36). When he is singled out he is referred to as God's friend (Isa. 41.8) and servant (Ps. 105.6), and in times of trouble the Israelites are to remember that though he was but one man, a multitude derives from him (Isa. 51.2). This picture is greatly expanded in the later books of the LXX. Sirach, for example, says: 'Abraham was the great father of a multitude of nations and no one has been found like him in glory' (44.19). He is praised for keeping the law, entering into a covenant with God and 'when he was tested he proved faithful' (44.20). Abraham's willingness to sacrifice Isaac acts as an inspiration to those facing martyrdom in the Maccabean period, confident in the belief that he will be there to welcome them into paradise (4 Macc. 13.17). In the light of Paul's focus on Genesis 15.6 ('Abraham believed God and it was reckoned to him as righteousness'), it is worth quoting 1 Maccabees 2.50–52 in full:

> Now, my children, show zeal for the law, and give your lives for the covenant of our ancestors. Remember the deeds of the ancestors, which they did in their generations; and you will receive great honour and an everlasting name. Was not Abraham found faithful when tested, *and it was reckoned to him as righteousness?*

This tendency to honour Abraham for his law-keeping and his faithfulness is taken further in the work known as *Jubilees* (*c.* 150 BCE). What stands out in *Jubilees* is that the 'testing' of Abraham now appears as the seventh of a sequence of tests in which Abraham proved faithful. The stories of the land and famine (Gen. 13), the wealth of kings (Gen. 14), the need to pass Sarah off as his sister (Gen. 12; 20), circumcision (Gen. 17) and Hagar and Ishmael (Gen. 16) are all regarded as 'tests' in which Abraham proves himself: 'Abraham was perfect with the Lord in everything that he did' (*Jub.* 23.10). Indeed, even though he lived before the law was given to Moses, he is shown to have observed the festivals and offered the prescribed sacrifices.

Abraham in James 2

A more modest eulogy to Abraham, but in the same tradition, occurs in the letter of James. It is still a matter of debate as to the relationship of this passage to Paul's writings, but at the very least it shows that Paul's views were not held by every branch of Christianity. James is concerned about consistency: do a person's deeds reflect their profession of faith? He illustrates his case by referring to Abraham's willingness to sacrifice Isaac:

> Was not our ancestor Abraham justified by works when he offered his son Isaac on the altar? You see that faith was active along with his works, and faith was brought to completion by the works. Thus the scripture was fulfilled that says, 'Abraham believed God, and it was reckoned to him as righteousness', and he was called the friend of God. You see that a person is justified by works and not by faith alone.
>
> (James 2.21–24)

Paul and Abraham

Where will Paul sit in this developing tradition? Will he accept the 'heroic' portrait and show that Christ was even more exalted, by virtue of his divinity? Or will he challenge it, perhaps drawing attention to those parts of the Genesis story that are less favourable, such as urging his wife to join Pharaoh's harem rather than risk danger to himself? To criticize Abraham would disenfranchise him from his fellow Jews, and yet the gospel he proclaims insists that 'all have sinned and fall short of the glory of God' (Rom. 3.23) and that 'death spread to all because all have sinned' (Rom. 5.12). Paul's arguments are often complex and intertwined with other texts and themes, but for convenience we will consider his use of Abraham under three headings. First, Paul's use of Genesis 15.6 ('Abraham believed God and it was reckoned to him as righteousness'); second, Paul's defence that Gentile Christians do not need to be circumcised to join the people of God, even though Abraham was; third, Paul's use of Abraham's sons, Isaac and Ishmael, as a clue to God's purposes of election, and also as an allegory of those whose lives are characterized by freedom or slavery.

Paul's use of Genesis 15.6

Both in Galatians 3 and Romans 4, Paul begins his exposition of Abraham by quoting Genesis 15.6 in the form, 'Abraham believed God, and it was reckoned to him as righteousness'. The argument of Galatians is that 'faith' is the characteristic that most defines Abraham's standing before God. As a result, the Gentile Christians, who are being excluded because they do not bear the physical mark of belonging to Abraham (i.e. circumcision), can legitimately be called 'descendants of Abraham' if they share his faith. The idiom behind the inclusive translation 'descendants of Abraham' is the expression 'son of', used literally of physical lineage but also of shared characteristics. Thus the author of Acts explains the meaning of the name Bar-nabas as 'son of encouragement' (Acts 4.36), which does not mean that his father's name was 'Encouragement' but that he manifests the virtue of 'encouragement'. In Galatians 3.7, Gentile Christians can rightly be called 'sons of Abraham' because they share his faith, even though they are not of his physical lineage.

> Just as Abraham '*believed* God, and it was reckoned to him as right-eousness,' so, you see, those who *believe* are the descendants of Abraham. And the scripture, foreseeing that God would justify the Gentiles by *faith*, declared the gospel beforehand to Abraham, saying, 'All the Gentiles shall be blessed in you.' For this reason, those who *believe* are blessed with Abraham who *believed*.
>
> (Gal. 3.6–9)

What is surprising about this argument, from a Gentile Christian's perspective, is that it seems to concede too much to Abraham. Paul begins the letter by describing Jesus Christ as the one who 'gave himself for our sins to set us free from the present evil age' (Gal. 1.3). In the verse immediately before the Genesis 15.6 quotation, he reminds the Galatians of two of the benefits of this: the work of the Spirit and the occurrence of miracles (Gal. 3.5). Would it not be more appropriate to say that Abraham's faith has similarities to Christian faith rather than the other way around? Perhaps, but that does not appear to be Paul's concern here, for in the next verse he states that the gospel was preached beforehand to Abraham, citing Genesis 12.3; 18.18 ('All the Gentiles shall be blessed in you'). Paul is not asserting that Abraham knew about the death and resurrection of Christ, but when God promised to bless all the clans (Gen. 12.3) or nations (Gen. 18.18) *in Abraham*, it was in effect a *protoevangelium* (preview of the gospel). This has now been realized in the death and resurrection of Christ, so that 'those who believe are blessed with Abraham who believed' (Gal. 3.9).

There has of course been an intervening problem. The law promised blessing for obedience and curse for disobedience (e.g. Deut. 28), and so Israel finds herself under a curse. Galatians 3.10–13 shows how Christ has removed that curse so that 'the blessing of Abraham might come to the Gentiles', which Paul equates with the reception of the Spirit (Gal. 3.14). The flow of the argument in Galatians 3.6–14 is that God's promise to bless the Gentiles in Abraham is being realized as Gentiles put their faith in Christ. Far from being excluded from God's people, they were included in the original promise.

Righteousness and justification, faith and belief

It is difficult to bring out in English the fact that the Greek words for righteousness and justification come from the same root (*dik-*), as do the words for faith and belief (*pist-*). So when Paul says that 'God would justify (*dikaioo*) the Gentiles by faith (*pistis*)', he is drawing on the words of Genesis 15.6: 'Abraham believed (*pisteuo*) God and it was reckoned to him as "righteousness"' (*dikaiosyne*). The issue is that English does not have verbs to correspond to the nouns 'righteousness' and 'faith'. There is thus a danger in thinking that Paul's doctrine of righteousness (often thought of as God's holy perfection) is different from his doctrine of justification (often thought of as forgiveness or acquittal) or his view of 'belief' is different from his view of 'faith'. One way around this would be to translate the verb *dikaioo* with the phrase 'to make righteous' and *pistis* with 'belief', but this can also be misleading: Galatians 3.8 would become 'God would make the Gentiles righteous by belief'; and Genesis 15.6 would become 'Abraham had faith in God and it was reckoned to him as justification'.[1]

Paul also quotes Genesis 15.6 in Romans 4.3, but here it is subject to detailed exposition. He first introduces a well-known principle from the field of employment: 'Now to one who works, wages are not reckoned as a gift but as something due' (Rom. 4.4). The connection is not obvious, though the verb 'to reckon' was sometimes used in commercial contexts. Paul develops the connection by asserting: 'But to one who without works trusts him who justifies the ungodly, such *faith is reckoned as righteousness*' (Rom. 4.5). Contrary to the developing 'heroic' tradition, Paul suggests that Abraham was 'without works' and that 'reckoned as righteousness' means the same thing as 'justifies the ungodly'.

Such an interpretative move could be seen as arbitrary, since it depends on Paul's introduction of an employment analogy, rather than a deduction from the actual text of Scripture. But he also uses a well-known exegetical device (known as *gezerah sewa*) whereby a word in one text is explained by its occurrence in another text. Psalm 32.2 is such a verse, using the key verb 'to reckon'. Paul quotes the text in the form: 'Blessed are those whose iniquities are forgiven, and whose sins are covered; blessed is the one against whom the Lord will not *reckon* sin.' On the surface, the two verses have little in common. Genesis 15.6 is about Abraham's acceptance of God's promise to provide him with descendants; Psalm 32.2 is David's lament over his sin. But David is talking about 'blessing', and the whole Abraham narrative is about God's promise of blessing. The reference to 'blessing' and the shared word 'reckon' suggests to Paul that the two verses are referring to the same thing. Thus he can deduce that 'David speaks of the blessedness of those to whom God reckons righteousness *apart from works*' (Rom. 4.6). In other words, having righteousness reckoned to oneself (Abraham) is equivalent to having one's sins forgiven (David).

Having put Abraham in the same position as the ungodly, Paul goes on to examine the structure of Abraham's faith. Who was the God that he believed in? It was a God 'who gives life to the dead and calls into existence the things that do not exist' (Rom. 4.17). This way of describing God allows Paul to connect Abraham's act of faith – namely, that God would give him descendants despite his wife's barrenness and his great age – with Christian faith, which believes that God raised Jesus from the dead. By believing that God could bring life from 'fertility-dead' parents, Abraham's faith has the same dynamic as Christian faith:

> No distrust made him waver concerning the promise of God, but he grew strong in his faith as he gave glory to God, being fully convinced that God was able to do what he had promised. Therefore his faith 'was reckoned to him as righteousness.' Now the words, 'it was reckoned to him', were written not for his sake alone, but for ours also. It will be reckoned to us who believe in him who raised Jesus our Lord from the dead, who was handed over to death for our trespasses and was raised for our justification.
>
> (Rom. 4.20–25)

Do 'justified sinners' need to be circumcised?

However, this does not provide an answer to the controversy that engulfed the early Church, namely whether such Gentile Christians should be required to submit to circumcision (Acts 15.1). There were strong reasons for suggesting that they should, for not only does the Genesis narrative state that circumcision was to be the sign of the covenant between God and Abraham, including his descendants (Gen. 17.10), it also specifically mentions foreigners (Gen. 17.12). If God is accepting Gentile Christians as 'children of Abraham', as Paul wishes to assert (Gal. 3.7), why should they not be circumcised as a *sign* of belonging to this new family? It would appear that those advocating Gentile circumcision had a strong case, based on Scripture, tradition and experience. Indeed, were not Jesus, the early disciples and even Paul himself all circumcised?

In the first half of Galatians, Paul only hints that this is the problem. When describing a meeting in Jerusalem – probably the same as the one described in Acts 15 – he notes that 'Titus, who was with me, was not compelled to be circumcised, though he was a Greek' (Gal. 2.3). However, when narrating a controversy concerning food laws, he accuses Peter of hypocrisy because he withdrew from the Gentiles 'for fear of the circumcision faction' (Gal. 2.12). Paul does not elaborate at this point, but in Galatians 5—6, we learn that this is the 'yoke of slavery' that Paul has been talking about. There are those who are insisting that Gentile Christians must be circumcised, and Paul challenges both their motives and their theology.

In Galatians 6.11–13, Paul gives two reasons why they are insisting on circumcision: to avoid being 'persecuted for the cross of Christ' and to 'boast about your flesh'. Both are somewhat obscure. The meaning of the first depends on whether the persecutors are thought to be Romans or Jews, or perhaps Jewish Christians. If it is the Romans, then the idea is that Gentile Christians could avoid persecution by coming under the umbrella of Judaism, which was regarded by Rome as a legal religion (*religio licita*). However, it is unlikely that the Romans would be interested in such distinctions and, since they regarded circumcision as an irrational mutilation, would hardly have been impressed by such an argument. If the persecutors were Jews, then the accusation is that the Jewish Christians were trying to demonstrate their loyalty to Judaism by making the Gentile Christians appear as God-fearers or Jewish proselytes. Such people were attracted to Judaism by its lofty monotheism and ethical standards but largely unwilling to be circumcised. In this case, boasting to fellow Jews that they had persuaded Gentiles to follow the law and submit to circumcision might have deflected criticism from their own particular Christian beliefs.

Paul's theological objections begin with the statement that 'if you let yourselves be circumcised, Christ will be of no benefit to you' (Gal. 5.2). It is noteworthy that Paul does not try and relate this to Abraham, who believed the promise *and* submitted to circumcision. Instead, he takes it as an indicator that the person submitting to circumcision wishes to orientate their life around law rather than Christ. He points out that circumcision was merely the beginning of covenant identity. The person who wishes to take this path is obliged to keep the whole law (Gal. 5.3), something even the Jews have not been able to manage (Gal. 6.13). Paul stated in Galatians 3.28 that 'There is no longer Jew or Greek, there is no longer slave or free, there is no longer male and female; for all of you are one in Christ Jesus.' He now applies this to circumcision: 'For in Christ Jesus neither circumcision nor uncircumcision counts for anything; the only thing that counts is faith working through love' (Gal. 5.6; cf. also Gal. 6.16).

When we turn to Romans, however, we find that Paul does attempt to justify his stance with respect to Abraham. Having cited Genesis 15.6 and explained it with reference to Psalm 32.2, Paul focuses on the Genesis story and asks whether Abraham was circumcised or uncircumcised when this righteousness was reckoned to him. The answer is obvious but Paul states it nonetheless: 'It was not after, but before he was circumcised' (Rom. 4.10). He then clarifies the purpose of circumcision, drawing particularly on Genesis 17.11, which refers to it as a 'sign of the covenant'. Paul introduces the word 'seal' in order to make the statement: 'He received the sign of circumcision as a *seal* of the righteousness that he had by faith while he was still uncircumcised' (Rom. 4.11). This is important, because those insisting on circumcision could also use a chronological argument: Abraham received the promise of God but was then commanded to submit to circumcision. Likewise, the Gentiles have received the promise of God – as evidenced by the gift of the Spirit – and should now submit to circumcision, as Abraham did. For Paul, the promise takes absolute priority and is received by faith or trust in the one doing the promising. The later act of circumcision is a sign *and* a seal of that covenant, but not its foundation.

However, as we shall see in the next section, one of Paul's concerns in Romans is to show that extending the promises to include Gentiles does not mean that God's promises to Israel have failed. For the sake of Gentile Christians, he draws out the consequences of Abraham's uncircumcision at the time of the promise: 'The purpose was to make him the ancestor of all who believe without being circumcised and who thus have righteousness reckoned to them' (Rom. 4.11). On the other hand, the fact that 13 years later (according to Genesis 16.16; 17.1) Abraham was circumcised means that he is also the 'ancestor of the circumcised who are not only circumcised but who also follow the example of the faith that our ancestor Abraham had before he was circumcised' (Rom. 4.12). So Genesis contains stories about Abraham before and after he was circumcised, which allows Paul to assert that he is the 'ancestor' of both Gentiles and Jews.

Abraham and his sons

The stories of Ishmael and Isaac provide material for a classic debate on the relationship between the one and the many. Having argued that Gentile Christians can rightly be called 'descendants of Abraham' because they share his faith, Paul uses a quasi-linguistic argument to show that Christ is the true fulfilment of the promise: 'Now the promises were made to Abraham and to his offspring (*sperma*); it does not say, "And to offsprings", as of many; but it says, "And to your offspring", that is, to one person, who is Christ' (Gal. 3.16). This is a strange argument for two reasons. First, having demonstrated that Gentile Christians are included in the promise of 'offspring' for Abraham, it appears counterproductive to argue now that in fact the promise refers to a single individual, namely Christ. Second, as a linguistic argument it is fallacious since *sperma* ('seed' or 'offspring') is a collective singular, meaning descendants. Not only is it false to say that the writer would have written 'offsprings' if a plurality was intended, the context also makes it quite clear that a plurality was intended. Abraham's 'offspring' will be like the stars of heaven (Gen. 15.5) or the sand on the seashore (Gen. 22.17). How can Paul think this argument is convincing?

The clue comes later in Galatians 3.29 (anticipated in 3.26): 'And if you belong to Christ, then you are Abraham's offspring, heirs according to the promise.' Paul's argument is not christological in the sense of demonstrating that Christ fulfils the Scriptures. Unlike Matthew's Gospel and Hebrews, Paul rarely seeks to prove that Christ is the Messiah because he fulfils messianic prophecies. As Hays has argued, it is more ecclesiological in the sense that Christ is both a singular and a corporate figure. Christians are 'in Christ'; that is, they have been incorporated into Christ's body, the Church.[2] So if Christ is the true 'offspring' (singular) of Abraham, Christians who are 'in Christ' are also recipients of the promise and thus qualify as Abraham's 'offspring' (plurality). There are therefore two arguments for why Gentile Christians can legitimately be called 'children of Abraham'. The first is that they share the leading characteristic of Abraham, namely his faith; the second is that they are 'in Christ', who is the 'offspring' of Abraham par excellence.

The more difficult question is the status of Paul's linguistic argument. There is certainly warrant in the scriptural narrative that 'offspring' can sometimes refer to a single person. Indeed, in Genesis 21.12–13 we have both uses side by side: 'for it is through Isaac that offspring [plural meaning] shall be named for you. As for the son of the slave woman, I will make a nation of him also, because he is your offspring [singular meaning].' Perhaps Paul's so-called linguistic argument has a tongue-in-cheek quality: by drawing attention to the singular form, even though it is clear from the context that a plurality is meant, he points his readers to a profound truth: that its fulfilment will be both singular (Christ) and corporate (the Church, those who are 'in Christ'). Or perhaps Tom Wright is correct in believing that Paul understands the promise of *sperma* ('seed') to mean 'family', as it does in Ezra 2.59. If so, then Paul's point is not that the promise of descendants actually referred to one person, namely Christ, but that the promise of a (singular) family is being realized 'in Christ'. In other words, since the original promise did not speak of 'families' in the plural, nor should the Church be divided into Jewish and Gentile 'families'.[3]

A different type of argument arises when Paul draws a contrast between two of Abraham's offspring, Ishmael and Isaac, in order to argue against those insisting on Gentile circumcision. Again, the form of the argument (Gal. 4.21–31) has been questioned but the thrust of it is clear. Ishmael and Isaac were both 'offspring' of Abraham but their origins were quite different. Ishmael was born to the slave woman Hagar, whereas Isaac was born to the free woman Sarah. Furthermore, Ishmael was a result of Abraham taking matters into his own hands (at Sarah's instigation) and so was born 'according to the flesh' (Gal. 4.23). In contrast, Isaac was a child of promise, something the Genesis narratives repeatedly emphasize. However, Ishmael is not abandoned by God but will also be a great nation (Gen. 21.13). Thus Paul sees in the two sons an allegory (he calls it this in Galatians 4.24), whereby the two sons/mothers represent two types of covenant, one marked by freedom and one marked by slavery. Not surprisingly, Paul applies the covenant of freedom to his Gentile converts and the covenant of slavery to those insisting on circumcision. It is therefore similar to his argument that Gentile Christians are rightly called 'children of Abraham' because they share his faith. Gentile Christians belong to the covenant of freedom because freedom characterizes their being 'in Christ' (and is evidenced by their experience of the Spirit), whereas those insisting on circumcision are characterized by slavery. Paul has, then, overturned the traditional interpretation (Jews are descended from Sarah and Gentiles from Hagar) by associating those who are insisting on circumcision (probably Jewish Christians) with Hagar:

For it is written that Abraham had two sons, one by a slave woman and the other by a free woman. One, the child of the slave, was born according to the flesh; the other, the child of the free woman, was born through the promise. Now this is an allegory: these women are two covenants. One woman, in fact, is Hagar, from Mount Sinai, bearing children for slavery. Now Hagar is Mount Sinai in Arabia and corresponds to the present Jerusalem, for she is in slavery with her children. But the other woman corresponds to the Jerusalem above; she is free, and she is our mother.

(Gal. 4.22–26)

Paul makes a further deduction from the Genesis story. When Sarah saw Ishmael 'playing' with Isaac, she said to Abraham: 'Cast out this slave woman with her son; for the son of this slave woman shall not inherit along with my son Isaac' (Gen. 21.10). We are told that Abraham was dismayed at this, but God instructed him to go along with it. Paul therefore takes this action to be the will of God and quotes the text as a command for the Gentile Christians to have nothing to do with those advocating circumcision. By their insistence on circumcision, they are 'children of the slave woman' and have no part in the inheritance of the free.

Paul's retelling of the story differs from the Genesis text in one important detail. Paul gives the rationale for the 'casting out' action as follows: 'But just as at that time the child who was born according to the flesh *persecuted* the child who was born according to the Spirit, so it is now also' (Gal. 4.29). There is nothing in the Genesis text that says that Ishmael persecuted Isaac. In fact the Hebrew text that has come down to us (MT) simply says that Sarah saw Ishmael 'playing'. The LXX (and Vulgate) add 'with Isaac', and most Bible translations adopt this as the most likely reading, assuming the words must have dropped out of the Hebrew text. It would appear that Paul deduced from Sarah's harsh reaction that 'playing' means 'making sport with' in a negative, perhaps even spiteful sense, which Paul interprets as persecution. If this seems arbitrary or underhand, it should be noted that the first-century Jewish historian, Josephus, makes the same deduction (*Ant.* 1.215), and something is required to explain Sarah's harsh response. One might also question whether insistence on circumcision constitutes persecution, though it might have been accompanied by other forms of intimidation. Perhaps the seriousness of the dispute – in Paul's eyes – has led him to deliberately exaggerate the implications of the Genesis story.

A third use of the 'two sons' comes in Romans 9. It would appear that Paul's mission to the Gentiles has led some to doubt his concern for his own people (Rom. 9.1), and even more importantly, whether the implication is that God has rejected them. Later in Romans 9, Paul will assert that even if God had behaved like this, it would not be the place of humans to criticize God (Rom. 9.21). However, at this point, Paul's concern is that the success of the Gentile mission and the relative failure of the Jewish mission could imply that God's promises to Abraham, Isaac and Jacob have failed. Not only would that besmirch God's character, it would also raise questions as to whether the Gentile Christians can put their trust/faith in such a God. Paul counters this by noting that even though Abraham had more than one son, the promise took the form: 'It is through Isaac that descendants shall be named for you' (Rom. 9.7). He can thus claim that 'not all Israelites truly belong to Israel', an argument he has already made in Romans 2.28–29:

> For a person is not a Jew who is one outwardly, nor is true circumcision something external and physical. Rather, a person is a Jew who is one inwardly, and real circumcision is a matter of the heart – it is spiritual and not literal. Such a person receives praise not from others but from God.

In Romans 9 he uses the language of 'flesh' and 'promise' (as in Galatians) rather than 'outwardly' and 'inwardly'. If descendants are promised through Isaac, then it 'means that it is not the children of the flesh who are the children of God, but the children of the promise are counted as descendants' (Rom. 9.8). Of course, the Jews would argue that since they are descended from Isaac, not Ishmael, they are children of the flesh *and* children of the promise. However, Paul's emphasis is not on natural lineage but on God's freedom to make choices in order to accomplish his purposes:

> Nor is that all; something similar happened to Rebecca when she had conceived children by one husband, our ancestor Isaac. Even before they had been born or had done anything good or bad (so that God's purpose of election might continue, not by works but by his call) she was told, 'The elder shall serve the younger.'
>
> (Rom. 9.10–12)

We will consider the rest of this argument in Chapter 4, but here we will summarize Paul's use of the Abraham narratives.

Conclusion

Since Abraham was responsible for instituting circumcision as a sign of the covenant (Gen. 17), it was perhaps necessary for Paul to demonstrate why this does not imply that his Gentile converts need to be circumcised. He does this by focusing on Genesis 15.6, making 'faith' the identity marker for belonging to God's people and noting (in Romans) that this promise came before circumcision. He also draws conclusions from the stories about Abraham's two sons, though his identification of those insisting on circumcision with Ishmael must have been truly shocking. It is possible that Paul had pondered the issue of promise and law prior to his Damascus-road experience, but his zeal for upholding the latter suggests that his interpretations are largely the result of a christological 'reconfiguration'. His mission to preach to Gentiles forced him back to the Scriptures to find the promise that Gentiles would be blessed in Abraham, but the Scriptures do not say that there is no need for such people to be circumcised. It is what God is currently doing that gives Paul this insight.

3

Paul and Moses

Introduction

If Abraham is the *founder* of the Jewish people, Moses is the figure that most defines the *nature* of Judaism. He is the central figure in Exodus–Deuteronomy, where he is mentioned 604 times, and frequently in the books that follow: Joshua (58 times); 1 and 2 Kings (10 times); 1 and 2 Chronicles (21 times). He is mentioned by name over 40 times in the Gospels, 20 times in Acts, 8 times in Paul and 11 times in Hebrews. He appears to Jesus in the transfiguration story (along with Elijah) and in Acts 7 and Hebrews 11 much space is devoted to retelling his story (Acts 7.20–44; Heb 11.23–29). He is principally remembered for three things: he led Israel out of Egypt; he gave Israel the law; and he was Israel's greatest prophet. He is celebrated in the Psalms as 'man of God' (Ps. 90.1), 'priest' (Ps. 99.6), 'servant' (Ps. 105.26) and 'chosen one' (Ps. 106.23), and Psalm 90 is attributed to him. According to Numbers 12.3 he was 'very humble, more so than anyone else on the face of the earth', and in Numbers 12.8 God declares that he speaks to Moses 'face to face' and that Moses 'beholds the form of the LORD'. Not surprisingly, a rich tradition of stories and accolades developed around Moses, and as we shall see, Paul uses the biblical and extra-biblical stories in a number of interesting ways.

Moses in the Pentateuch

The story of Moses begins with his mother hiding him in a basket among the reeds to protect him from the Pharaoh's decree that all Hebrew boys should be thrown into the Nile (Exod. 2.1–3). He is rescued by Pharaoh's daughter, which provides the explanation for his name, 'Moses', which has the same consonants as the verb 'to draw out' (Exod. 2.10). In Exodus 3 he receives his commission (burning bush) to lead the Israelites out of Egypt. Since the Pharaoh – unsurprisingly – refuses, Moses brings upon the Egyptians a series of plagues

(Exod. 7—10), culminating in the death of their firstborn (Exod. 12). On that night, later celebrated as Passover, Moses leads the people out of Egypt and miraculously crosses the sea of reeds (the LXX mistakenly calls this the Red Sea, which is too far south), while the Egyptian armies drown. This victory is celebrated in the 'Song of Moses' (Exod. 15), which plays an important role in later tradition.

Having led the people out of Egypt and across the sea, Moses leads them into the Sinai desert, where he receives the Ten Commandments (Exod. 20), along with a host of other laws and details of three great festivals that the people are to observe (Passover, Pentecost, Tabernacles). While Moses is up the mountain, the people persuade Aaron to make them a golden calf to be their god (Exod. 32). Moses is furious and destroys the tablets of the law, grinds the golden calf into dust, mixes it with water and forces the Israelites to drink it. In Exodus 34, Moses ascends the mountain again to receive the commandments, and in an incident that Paul will discuss in 2 Corinthians 3, finds that his face is glowing because he has been in the presence of God (or perhaps because he is carrying the commandments). Curiously, when the 'ten words' are listed (Exod. 34.11–28), they bear little relation to the Ten Commandments of Exodus 20.

The book of Leviticus is mainly concerned with ritual and purity laws, including instructions for the day of Atonement (Lev. 23) and the jubilee year (every 50 years), when property reverts to its original owners (Lev. 25). The book of Numbers – so-called because it begins and ends with a census – outlines the 40 years in the wilderness, where all those, except Caleb and Joshua, over 20 years old died because of their rebellion (Num. 14). In a further incident, the people complain that they have no water, and God tells Moses to strike the rock with his staff, from which water pours forth. However, Moses has apparently behaved improperly, for God tells him that he too will not enter the promised land, though the nature of his fault is obscure (Num. 20.12; cf. Num. 27.12–14). The book ends with the new generation of Israelites on the brink of the promised land.

The book of Deuteronomy (lit. 'second law') consists of three speeches of Moses that summarize the journey so far, repeat many of the laws – sometimes in slightly different form – and give instructions for the settlement. Perhaps the most famous are the instruction to 'love the LORD your God with all your heart, and with all your soul, and with all your might' (Deut. 6.5) and the text quoted in Jesus' temptation (Matt./Luke): 'one does not live by bread alone, but by every word that comes from the mouth of the LORD' (Deut. 8.4). The final chapters are of particular importance to Paul and consist of a list of blessings and curses for obedience and disobedience (Deut. 27—30), another 'Song of Moses' (Deut. 32), the 'blessing of Moses' (Deut. 33) and an account of his death (Deut. 34), which ends with this eulogy:

> Never since has there arisen a prophet in Israel like Moses, whom the LORD knew face to face. He was unequalled for all the signs and wonders that the LORD sent him to perform in the land of Egypt, against Pharaoh and all his servants and his entire land, and for all the mighty deeds and all the terrifying displays of power that Moses performed in the sight of all Israel.
>
> (Deut. 34.10–12)

Moses in Jewish tradition

It is perhaps hard to imagine how later tradition could enlarge on this assessment, but in the words of Jeremias: 'his person is now panegyrically magnified, and his life and work are surrounded by an almost innumerable host of legends.'[1] Thus he was not only Israel's lawgiver but the inventor of the alphabet, which the Greeks learnt by way of the Phoenicians (Eupolemus). Indeed, according to Aristobulus, the Greek philosophers (Plato, Socrates, Pythagoras) and the Greek poets (Homer, Hesiod) borrowed from Moses. According to Artapanus he was a great inventor (ships, weapons), architect, politician, man of education and culture and worthy of divine honour. Philo devotes a whole treatise to him (*Vita Mosis*), emphasizing his attributes, both philosophical (Moses' curiosity about the burning bush was a quest to understand cause and effect) and contemplative (40 days of fasting in the presence of God). He calls him 'the perfect man'. Though at times he comes close to calling Moses 'divine', Philo is clear that no human can comprehend the divine essence without revelation. What is unique about Moses is that he is the only person who is sufficient to receive God's revelation.

The biblical stories are also subject to embellishment (*haggada*) in the tradition of the 'heroic romance' (Jeremias). So according to Josephus, Moses' birth had been prophesied by an Egyptian seer; as a child he wore the Pharaoh's crown; and he led the Egyptian army against the Ethiopians (*Ant.* 2.205ff.). Concerning his death, some rabbis ascribe an atoning significance to it, particularly on behalf of those who died in the wilderness generation or are buried outside Israel. There is a legend about the archangel Michael contending with the devil for the body of Moses, a tradition that is also found in the New Testament book of Jude (v. 9). Josephus also knows of a tradition where Moses was taken up into heaven (like Enoch and Elijah), though he himself agrees with Deuteronomy 34 that Moses died and was buried. Later Christian writers believed that a work known as the *Assumption of Moses* spoke of Moses' assumption into heaven, though this part of the book is no longer extant. As Scott Hafemann notes, it is impossible to construct a single coherent account from these traditions, but they do provide us with a background of ideas with which Paul might have been agreeing, disagreeing or simply unfamiliar.[2]

Paul and Moses

Moses and Pharaoh

Paul does not refer to the early life of Moses, but in Romans 9.15–18 he uses the confrontation between Moses and Pharaoh to extend his argument, begun in Romans 9.6, that 'not all Israelites truly belong to Israel'. God's choice of Isaac is further illustrated by referring to Jacob and Esau. Quoting the texts of Genesis 25.21 ('The elder shall serve the younger') and Malachi 1.2–3 ('I have loved Jacob, but I have hated Esau'), Paul argues that God's choices are independent of human action for they were made 'before they had been born or had done anything good or bad (so that God's purpose of election might continue, not by works but by his call)' (Rom. 9.11–12). Indeed, God can even use Israel's enemies to further his purposes. 'For the scripture says to Pharaoh, "I have raised you up for the very purpose of showing my power in you, so that my name may be proclaimed in all the earth"' (Rom. 9.17, quoting Exod. 9.16). Paul's expression that 'scripture says to Pharaoh' is interesting. A more accurate description would be that 'Scripture reports that God told Moses to say to Pharaoh', and it is possible that Paul means this. However, there are other passages where Scripture is personified as 'speaking' (Gal. 3.8), and Richard Hays has argued that this is deliberate: Paul does not quote Scripture because it is a distant witness to events happening now; he quotes Scripture because it is a living voice: 'This time-spanning speech of the text is a crucial attribute; the text is reckoned as a knowing voice that has the power to address the present out of the past – or to address the past about the present, in such a way that readers, overhearing, may reconceive the present.'[3] We will say more about Hays's 'hermeneutical theory' later in the book.

God's choice of Isaac and Jacob focuses on God's gracious purposes, which is confirmed by a quotation from Exodus 33.19 in the form: 'I will have mercy on whom I have mercy, and I will have compassion on whom I have compassion.' But the introduction of Pharaoh brings another element to the discussion: God's purposes also involve *hardening*, so that some are bound to resist God – 'So then he has mercy on whomsoever he chooses, and he hardens the heart of whomsoever he chooses' (Rom. 9.18). Paul is aware of the moral difficulty that this raises – 'You will say to me then, "Why then does he still find fault? For who can resist his will?"' – but finds it groundless. It is not for the pot to question why the potter does what he does. Indeed, even if God's plan were to predestine some to destruction and some to glory (Rom. 9.22–23), it would still be his right to do so (the hypothetical 'what if God?', which begins the sentence in 9.22, is never finished, and it remains a matter of debate as to whether Paul thinks that God has in fact done this or not).

The theme of divine hardening is picked up in Romans 11, but with a different subject. Here Paul is explaining why many in Israel have not believed in Christ. He refers to those who have believed as the 'elect', while 'the rest were hardened' (Rom. 11.7). However, as in the story of Moses and Pharaoh ('so that my name may be proclaimed in all the earth'), this hardening is part of a larger purpose, which he states in Romans 11.25: 'a hardening has come upon part of Israel, until the full number of the Gentiles has come in'. Thus the story of Moses and Pharaoh has become paradigmatic for God accomplishing his gracious purposes through those who are – currently – opposing him.

Moses and Sinai

Paul only mentions Sinai in the Sarah and Hagar allegory of Galatians 4, where the slave woman Hagar is identified with those who are seeking to enslave the Gentile Christians by insisting that they keep the law. Paul lays the ground for this identification by stating that Hagar is from Mount Sinai, a clear reference to the giving of the law. There does not appear to be any textual evidence that Hagar was from this region, and most scholars accept that this is simply part of the allegory. What is not clear is whether Paul is criticizing the law itself or the *misuse* of it by those who are seeking to impose it on Gentiles. Earlier in Galatians 3.19–20 Paul says three things about the giving of the law: it was added because of (lit. 'in favour of') transgressions; it was given until the promised offspring should come; and it was ordained through angels by a mediator. We will discuss the first two of these in our next chapter ('Paul and the law'), but the third appears to reflect a tradition that angels were present at the top of Mount Sinai and were responsible for giving the law to Moses. Acts 7.53 knows the same tradition ('You are the ones that received the law as ordained by angels'), and it is possible that it originates from the LXX rendering of Deuteronomy 33.2 (lit. 'The Lord has come from Sinai...on his right hand were his angels with him'). It is probably an attempt to avoid anthropomorphism (describing God in human terms), and so it is God's angels who hand over the law; Paul may mean no more than this. On the other hand, some scholars believe that Paul is so intent on undermining the position of his opponents that he is deliberately distancing God from the law (God – angels – Moses – Israel). This is possible, but Drane's claim that it is a 'categorical denial of the divine origin of the Torah' seems unlikely in the light of the positive statements Paul makes about the law elsewhere.[4]

Allegory and typology

Allegory was an important mode of interpretation in the ancient world and was particularly significant to those who regarded certain writings as sacred. The rationale was simple: if the divine had inspired these texts, then every sentence, word and letter must have profound meaning. For Philo of Alexandria, this meant discovering all manner of philosophical propositions in the Pentateuch. For the authors of the Dead Sea Scrolls, it meant finding prophecies of their community's history and key personnel in the prophets (see Appendix 3 for some short abstracts). For the early Church, prompted by Paul's allegory of Sarah and Hagar and some of Jesus' parables (vineyard; sower), it meant finding Christian doctrine in all manner of texts. Hence Augustine famously interpreted the parable of the Good Samaritan by a series of identifications: the man who went from Jerusalem was Adam; he was robbed of his immortality; the Samaritan was

Jesus; the animal that took him to the inn was belief in the incarnation; the inn was the Church; the innkeeper was the apostle Paul! However, the Reformers reacted against this kind of interpretation and insisted that there must be some warrant in the text for making such identifications. Later, the term typology was coined as a better explanation for the way the New Testament authors used the Old Testament. It differed from allegory in two ways: first, while the original context and meaning is transcended, it is not ignored; and second, there is a salvation-history logic that connects the two events. Thus although Paul's identification of his opponent with Hagar seems arbitrary, the original story *is* clearly about the origins of two peoples.[5]

Moses and the Israelite rebellion

The early Christians lived in a world that was thought to be governed by gods and spirits. This not only presented difficulties in attending public events, which would begin with an offering of incense to the gods (and at times the Emperor), but also for what was on sale in the market. Meat would almost certainly have been involved in some ceremony at the time of slaughter, and a debate had arisen in Corinth as to whether Christians could eat such meat. Some were arguing that since Christians believed in one God, such 'gods' or 'idols' had no real existence and hence Christians had nothing to fear from eating such meat. In 1 Corinthians 8 Paul appears to endorse this view. However, in 1 Corinthians 10 he also identifies with the opposite view, that pagan sacrifices are evil and Christians should have nothing to do with them. Hence he declares that while 'idols' are nothing, such sacrifices are in fact being offered to demons rather than God (1 Cor. 10.20). And his warning against participating in such practices is drawn from the wilderness rebellions:

Do not become idolaters as some of them did; as it is written, 'The people sat down to eat and drink, and they rose up to play.' We must not indulge in sexual immorality as some of them did, and twenty-three thousand fell in a single day. We must not put Christ to the test, as some of them did, and were destroyed by serpents. And do not complain as some of them did, and were destroyed by the destroyer.

(1 Cor. 10.7–10)

In rapid succession Paul alludes to four of the wilderness rebellions. The explicit quotation – 'The people sat down to eat and drink, and they rose up to play' (rsv) – agrees exactly with the lxx of Exodus 32.6, and refers to the incident of the golden calf, where 3,000 people died (Exod. 32.28). The mention of the day when 23,000 died because of sexual immorality is almost certainly a reference to Numbers 25.1–10, though the figure that has come down to us (mt and lxx) is 24,000. Since there seems to be no particular reason why Paul would change the number, it is possible that he knew a different form of the text – or his memory let him down. The reference to being destroyed by serpents most likely refers to Numbers 21.5–6, while the accusation of complaining – using the Greek word *gonguzo* – could refer to a number of incidents (Num. 11.1; 14.27; 17.6).

On the surface, Paul's argument looks like a simple analogy: just as God punished the Israelites for idolatry, so he will punish you. But two factors indicate that it is more complicated than that. First, Paul says: 'These things happened to them to serve as an example, and they were written down to instruct us, on whom the ends of the ages have come' (1 Cor. 10.11). There is a progression here: first, they happened as examples to their fellow Israelites; second, they were written down so that they could act as examples to future generations, including us; third, they apply specifically to us because we are the generation 'on whom the ends of the ages have come'. This expression is linked to the common Jewish idea of 'the present age' and 'the age to come', but Paul adds the sense of 'finality' or 'ending'. The Christians are living in 'the last times', that period to which all of Scripture points, and thus, in Hays's words: 'all God's dealings with Israel in the past – as recounted in Scripture – must have pointed toward the present apocalyptic moment. If God was authoring the sacred story, then all the story's narrative patterns must foreshadow the experience of the community that has now encountered the apocalypse [lit. 'unveiling'] of God's grace.'[6]

Second, Paul's understanding that he is living in this 'apocalyptic moment' allows him to reinterpret the scriptural narrative, so that the Israelites are said to have 'put Christ to the test'. Of course Exodus and Numbers do not say this and no interpreter before the time of Christ could have deduced it. As we shall see in the next section, Paul believes that a veil has been lifted (2 Cor. 3.14–16), which is why he is able to see things in Scripture that were not previously seen.

Precisely how he understood Christ's pre-incarnate activity is not clear. Anthony Hanson believed that Paul envisaged Christ actively involved in Israel's history and referred to 1 Corinthians 10.4 as proof: 'For they drank from the spiritual rock that followed them, and the rock was Christ.'[7] Other scholars think this is too literal and prefer an explanation akin to later Trinitarian thought. If Christ is the eternal son of God, then actions of God are also actions of Christ. On this view, Paul was not saying that Christ was literally a 'moveable fountain' but that Israel's source of refreshment was ultimately God/Christ.

What is clear is that Paul is reinterpreting Scripture in ways that were not possible prior to the Christ-event. This is clear in the verses leading up to the statement that 'the rock was Christ'. Thus Paul can say that the Israelites 'were baptized into Moses' as they crossed the sea, and describes their diet as 'spiritual food' and 'spiritual drink' (1 Cor. 10.2–4). Since he will discuss the Lord's supper in 1 Corinthians 11, the rationale for calling the wilderness food 'spiritual' is to form a parallel with the bread and wine of the Christian celebration. And the phrase 'baptized into Moses' is obviously coined as a parallel to 'baptized into Christ' (Rom. 6.3; Gal. 3.27). It is because of such uses of Scripture as these that some scholars have turned to literary theory to account for how they work. Paul does not tell us which aspects of being 'baptized into Christ' – forgiveness, reception of the Spirit, incorporation into the Church – apply to Moses and the Israelites; it is left to the reader, in community with other readers and guided by the Spirit, to work it out.

A further feature of Paul's use of Scripture here is the idea that the rock that spouted water in Numbers 20 followed them on their wanderings. From the above, one might suggest that this is another example of Paul finding new meanings in Scripture, but in this case it is also found in a Jewish legend:

> And so the well which was with the Israelites in the wilderness was a rock, the size of a large round vessel, surging and gurgling upward, as from the mouth of this little flask, rising with them up onto the mountains, and going down with them into the valleys. Wherever the Israelites would encamp, it made camp with them, on a high place, opposite the entry to the Tent of Meeting.[8]

The written form of this legend dates from about 400 CE, but Anthony Hanson argues that it was hardly borrowed from Paul. It is more likely that both Paul and the author of the legend are drawing on a common source, which attempted to answer the question: What did the Israelites drink when they left Kadesh?

Ministry of Moses and Paul contrasted

In 2 Corinthians 3, Paul continues a defence of his ministry by contrasting it with that of Moses. He begins by stating that he does not need letters of recommendation to prove his authenticity because the Corinthians themselves are his letter, a letter not 'written with ink but with the Spirit of the living God' (2 Cor. 3.3).[9] However, he follows this contrast with an unmistakable reference to the law when he says: 'not on tablets of stone but on tablets of human hearts'. Since he goes on to say that he is a minister of a 'new covenant' (2 Cor. 3.6), it is likely that he has Jeremiah 31.33 in mind, where God promises: 'I will put my law within them, and I will write it on their hearts; and I will be their God, and they shall be my people.' It is not clear, from Paul or Jeremiah, if this is the same law that was given at Sinai or a different law – perhaps love of God and neighbour. What Paul does say is that 'the letter kills, but the Spirit gives life' (2 Cor. 3.6).[10]

We saw in Romans 5 that Paul contrasts the effects of Adam's disobedience (death, judgement, condemnation) with Christ's obedience (life, justification, righteousness). Now he contrasts the effects of Moses' ministry of the law (death, condemnation) with that of the Spirit (life, justification). If there was doubt about whether Paul was disparaging the law in Galatians 3.19, there can be no doubt when he calls it a 'ministry of death' (2 Cor. 3.7). Of course, it would be easy to argue both from the wilderness wanderings and the various exiles that the blessings and curses promised in the law did in fact result in death. In that sense the law's promise of blessing has been entirely hypothetical, for 'all have sinned and fall short of the glory of God' (Rom. 3.23). But Paul's criticism of the law appears to go deeper than the failure of people to keep it:

> Now if the ministry of death, chiselled in letters on stone tablets, came in glory so that the people of Israel could not gaze at Moses' face because of the glory of his face, a glory now set aside, how much more will the ministry of the Spirit come in glory? For if there was glory in

the ministry of condemnation, much more does the ministry of justification abound in glory! Indeed, what once had glory has lost its glory because of the greater glory; for if what was set aside came through glory, much more has the permanent come in glory!

(2 Cor. 3.7–11)

Paul seems to have got stuck on the word 'glory'! He is quite happy to acknowledge that there was a glory associated with the giving of the law, as he must if he takes the Exodus stories seriously. But this glory has been overwhelmingly surpassed by the glory of Christ, a glory in which Christians participate: 'And all of us, with unveiled faces, seeing the glory of the Lord as though reflected in a mirror, are being transformed into the same image from one degree of glory to another' (2 Cor. 3.18). Even so, it is still not clear why this warrants the derogatory 'ministry of death' and 'ministry of condemnation'.

Paul's answer focuses on a perplexing detail of the Exodus story, that when Moses was not conversing with God he would wear a veil over his face. One might have expected the opposite, for Exodus 33.20 says that no one can see God and live. However, the purpose of the veil in the story is connected with the fact that when Moses was in the presence of God, his face would glow (Exod. 34.29, 35). Since we are told that when Moses came down from the mountain the Israelites were afraid at the sight of his glowing face (Exod. 34.30), one might think that this is the reason for his practice of veiling. But the explanation in verse 34 does not bear this out, for after Moses had been in God's presence he would first tell the Israelites what God had commanded and only then put on the veil. As it stands, the text is obscure, and Paul offers an interpretation of it: 'Since, then, we have such a hope, we act with great boldness [or openness], not like Moses, who put a veil over his face to keep the people of Israel from gazing at the end of the glory that was being set aside' (2 Cor. 3.12–13). Paul makes several points here. First, he interprets Moses' action not as a kindness to the Israelites but as a lack of openness; Moses was trying to conceal something. Second, what he was trying to conceal was the temporary nature of the glowing (glory). As Watson notes, if Moses' face glowed in the presence of God and was still glowing when he explained God's commandments to them, then the only thing that the veil accomplished was to prevent the Israelites ever seeing Moses without his face glowing. And this could have given the false impression that the glowing was permanent. Thus although it is not explicit in the Exodus story, Paul finds here a parable of how the Israelites were kept from the knowledge that the law (and its glory) was temporary. Such a reading clearly springs from Paul's experience of the glory of Christ, but Watson argues that it is not simply an imposition on the text: 'Paul seeks to establish his position not just on the basis of prior dogmatic commitments, but also by way of an exegesis of selected texts from the law and the prophets which seem to him to show that his understanding of the law coincides with the law's own self-understanding – even if this self-understanding must be sought not on the surface of the texts but in their anomalies and gaps.'[11]

Moses and the righteousness that comes from faith

In Romans 10.5–13, Paul cites texts from Leviticus 18.5 and Deuteronomy 30.11–14, which state that the purpose of the law was to bring life ('the person who does these things will live by them') and was accessible ('The word is near you, on your lips and in your heart'). Deuteronomy 30 looks beyond a time of exile to a time when God will 'circumcise your heart and the heart of your descendants, so that you will love the LORD your God with all your heart and with all your soul, in order that you may live' (Deut. 30.6). However, when Deuteronomy 30.11 speaks of 'today', it appears to suggest that this accessibility has always been the case:

> Surely, this commandment that I am commanding you *today* is not too hard for you, nor is it too far away. It is not in heaven, that you should say, 'Who will go up to heaven for us, and get it for us so that we may hear it and observe it?' Neither is it beyond the sea, that you should say, 'Who will cross to the other side of the sea for us, and get it for us so that we may hear it and observe it?' No, the word is very near to you; it is in your mouth and in your heart for you to observe.
>
> (Deut. 30.11–14)

Paul changes the quest from ascending to heaven and crossing the sea, to the more logical ascending to heaven and descending to the abyss; but the more significant change is that he identifies the nearness and accessibility of the law with the gospel that he preaches. In an exegesis that resembles that of the Qumran commentators (see the text box below and Appendix 3), he takes each phrase and identifies it with an aspect of the gospel (indicated by parenthesis in the NRSV):

> 'Do not say in your heart, "Who will ascend into heaven?"' (that is, to bring Christ down) 'or "Who will descend into the abyss?"' (that is, to bring Christ up from the dead). But what does it say? 'The word is near you, on your lips and in your heart' (that is, the word of faith that we proclaim); because if you confess with your lips that Jesus is Lord and believe in your heart that God raised him from the dead, you will be saved.
>
> (Rom. 10.6–9)

If Paul is focusing on the future aspect of Deuteronomy 30, then identifying these words with the gospel is understandable. The time when God will circumcise hearts is now, and Paul's preaching of the gospel is the means by which it is accomplished. But what has puzzled commentators is the way that he introduces the two quotations. Leviticus 18.5 is introduced as the words of Moses – 'Moses writes concerning the righteousness that comes from the law' – but Deuteronomy 30.12–14 is introduced as the words of 'the righteousness that comes from faith' (Rom. 10.6). Paul has elsewhere personified Scripture as speaking (Gal. 3.8), but here it is something called 'the righteousness that comes from faith' that speaks. Testimony to this 'righteousness that comes from faith' has already come from Abraham (Rom. 4.3) and Habakkuk (Rom. 1.17), and now it comes from Moses, assuming that Paul understands Deuteronomy 30.12–14 as the words of Moses. This is a highly controversial passage that we will discuss further in Chapter 4.

Dead Sea Scrolls

In 1947 a shepherd boy threw a stone into a cave at Qumran, near the Dead Sea, and discovered a pot containing an ancient scroll. Excavations followed, and ten more caves were discovered, amounting to a small library of biblical texts, community rules, commentaries and hymns. This extraordinary discovery revealed a Jewish community that had separated from Jerusalem and settled in the desert to await God's act of judgement on the 'sons of darkness', and salvation for the 'sons of light' (themselves). They saw the origins of their community, its history and key personnel predicted in Scripture, and thus offer a significant parallel to Paul's use of Scripture. One of the discoveries was a line-by-line commentary on the first two chapters of Habakkuk, where the text was followed by the word *pesher* ('interpreted'), and then a comment that linked the text to the contemporary situation. One of the first scholars to compare this with Paul's use of Scripture was Earle Ellis: 'Taken as a whole, the Pauline citations reflect in substantial measure a *pesher*-type moulding of the text which in some cases is determinative for the NT application of the passage.'[12] Also of importance was the discovery of biblical texts almost 1,000 years older than what we previously possessed, demonstrating that the Hebrew text existed in a number of forms in the first century. The scrolls are categorized according to which cave they were found in (1Q, 2Q...11Q), and short extracts can be found in Appendix 3.

Conclusion

It would appear that Moses is an ambiguous figure for Paul. He speaks to God face to face, but his use of a veil is interpreted as a lack of openness. Indeed, Paul refers to the giving of the commandments as a 'ministry of death', a truly shocking idea for Paul's fellow Jews. He can quote Moses' words in Deuteronomy 30.12–14 (as he would have understood it) concerning the nearness and accessibility of God's word, and even identify his own preaching with them. But he then appears to distance Moses from the words by referring to their author as the 'righteousness that comes from faith'. Moses was remembered by the Jewish people as both prophet and lawgiver, but it is his prophetic voice that Paul claims to have heard in Scripture. As we shall see in the next chapter, his voice as lawgiver is far more troublesome for Paul's Gentile mission.

4

Paul and the law

Introduction

Alongside Paul's specific quotations from the Pentateuch there has been a huge debate about his overall attitude to the law. Sometimes he speaks in glowing terms: the law is spiritual (Rom. 7.14), comes from God (Rom. 3.2) and was written down for our sake (1 Cor. 9.10). At other times, he forbids circumcision (Gal. 5.2), questions the law's divine origins (Gal. 3.19) and calls it a 'ministry of death' (2 Cor. 3.7). The early Church explained this by dividing the law into moral laws and ceremonial laws. It argued that Christ had fulfilled the ceremonial or ritual laws by his sacrificial death, and so they are no longer in force. However, the moral law, as exemplified by the Ten Commandments, has abiding value as the expression of God's will for humankind. It was endorsed by Jesus (Mark 10.19f.) and Paul (Rom. 13.9f.) and remains the standard for human behaviour. However, there are at least two difficulties with this as an overall explanation for Paul's view of the law. First, there is no hint that Paul made such a division. Indeed, the Ten Commandments contain the command to observe the Sabbath, something Paul apparently sees as a matter of individual conscience (Rom. 14.5). Second, when Paul says that the 'letter kills, but the Spirit gives life' (2 Cor. 3.6–7), his description – 'chiselled in letters on stone tablets' – is clearly referring to the Ten Commandments. Thus a division between moral and ceremonial does not explain Paul's view of the law.

During the Reformation another explanation became prominent. Paul's critique of the law was not so much with the law itself but with the attempt to use it to gain favour with God. Drawing a parallel with the medieval church practice of selling indulgences, Luther argued that the Jews of Paul's day were seeking to *earn* their salvation by scrupulously keeping the law. Paul saw that such a quest was impossible because it was always defeated by human sin. That is why

God sent Jesus to die for sins and open up a new way to be right with God. This way was the way of faith, as exemplified by Genesis 15.6 ('Abraham believed God and it was reckoned to him as righteousness') and Habakkuk 2.4 ('The righteous by faith will live'). This explains why Paul can make both positive and negative statements about the law. Indeed, in order to further his mission he is quite happy to live like a Jew in order to reach Jews, and live like a Gentile in order to reach Gentiles (1 Cor. 9.20f.). But when circumcision is being demanded of his Gentile converts, he regards it as a betrayal of the gospel, for it is effectively making a human action a *condition* for salvation.

This theme of 'justification by faith alone' or, more correctly, 'justification by grace through faith' has not only been used to explain Paul, it has also been a potent critique of 'legalism'. Its strength lies in its simplicity. If human beings are sinful and caught up in the human condition of sinfulness, then there is nothing they can do to *earn* salvation. The only solution is to accept the grace that is on offer. Thus any religious practices that suggest that certain actions are *necessary* for salvation are categorized as 'salvation by works', whereas Paul believed in 'salvation by faith'. Even the sacraments of baptism and Eucharist must not be seen as *necessary* for salvation, though they can act as vehicles of God's grace. In the hands of Rudolf Bultmann even the desire for 'right doctrine' comes under the critique of 'works', for it is replacing absolute dependence on God (faith) with the necessity to hold to a particular form of words.[1]

However, it is this simplicity that has also come under attack. Nowhere in Galatians does Paul even hint that circumcision and food laws would be fine if the motive of the Gentile Christians was gratitude rather than an attempt to earn salvation. And the description of Judaism as a 'works religion' does not fit easily with many statements in the Old Testament that the law was viewed as a gift from God. As the author of Psalm 19.7–9 says: 'The law of the LORD is perfect, reviving the soul; the decrees of the LORD are sure, making wise the simple; the precepts of the LORD are right, rejoicing the heart; the commandment of the LORD is clear, enlightening the eyes; the fear of the LORD is pure, enduring for ever; the ordinances of the LORD are true and righteous altogether.' The whole of Psalm 119 (176 verses) is a eulogy to the benefits of the law. There is no hint that the law is a burden or a way of earning salvation.

The New Perspective on Paul

Jewish scholars have frequently made these points, but it was Ed Sanders who initiated a rethinking of the works–faith dichotomy, which has become known as the New Perspective on Paul or simply the New Perspective. In his book, *Paul and Palestinian Judaism*,[2] Sanders devotes some 400 pages to examining every form of first-century Judaism to which we have evidence, and declares that none of them believed that keeping the law was a means of earning salvation. Indeed, Jewish identity ran in quite the opposite direction. God had brought the Israelites out of Egypt – an act of grace – and entered into a covenant with them. All future Jews are born into this covenant; there is no question of having to earn their way into it.

The Greek word for law is *nomos*, and Sanders coined the term 'covenantal nomism' as a description of Jewish belief. It begins with grace, God's free choice to rescue Israel from Egypt and enter into covenant with her. As Deuteronomy 9.6 says: 'Know, then, that the LORD your God is not giving you this good land to occupy because of your righteousness; for you are a stubborn people.' God's choice of Israel is an act of grace and nothing to do with 'merit'. But in order to maintain this covenant, God gave Israel the law, a set of precepts and statutes for how they should relate to one another and how they should relate to God. It is to be noted that part of this law concerns what to do when sin disrupts this relationship. On Israel's side, they are to offer the prescribed sacrifices: 'If anyone of the ordinary people among you sins' (Lev. 4.27). On God's side, he vows to accept the sacrifices as a 'covering' for sin so that the covenant can be maintained: 'Thus the priest shall make atonement on your behalf for the sin that you have committed, and you shall be forgiven' (Lev. 4.35). That is why Paul can describe his status under the law as 'blameless' (Phil. 3.6). He was not claiming to be perfect, but when he did sin he followed the law's prescriptions for dealing with it. Sanders, in his analysis of the Jewish documents, suggests that the Jews thought of the law as the means by which they maintained the covenant ('staying in') rather than an attempt to earn something ('getting in').

Sanders notes that this has parallels with Paul's thought but does not think it gets to the heart of the matter. For Paul, salvation comes through dying and rising with Christ, not through a renewed covenant. But others have been more impressed with the parallels. The Reformation was correct to emphasize the priority of grace, but had neglected the other side of the covenant. In Paul's thought, God's grace is not only met by faith but also obedience (Rom. 1.5). Paul continually urges his congregations to live a life worthy of the gospel, and can even speak of rewards: 'So let us not grow weary in doing what is right, for we will reap at harvest time, if we do not give up' (Gal. 6.9). It is true that the obedience that Paul looked for was more aptly described by Leviticus 19.18 – 'you shall love your neighbour as yourself' – than the detailed prescriptions of the law. But the pattern of his thought was 'covenantal nomism', an act of grace that demands a response of faith and obedience. Paul's 'problem' with the law was that it is not the form of obedience that God requires of Gentiles.

These ideas were taken up by James Dunn.[3] He sees the controversies in Romans and Galatians not as a debate about Jewish self-righteousness ('getting in') but about Jewish privilege ('not wanting anyone else to get in'). He thus offers an explanation for why the points of dispute in Galatians are circumcision and food laws. These were the things that marked Jews as different from non-Jews. They were the visible signs that they belonged to God and were seeking to be faithful to his covenant. Indeed, a century or so before Paul there had been a sustained attempt to force Jews to give up such customs and assimilate. Some did, but the faithful among them would rather face death than betray God's covenant (the stories can be found in the LXX books of Maccabees). The so-called Judaizers were not demanding circumcision and food laws because they thought such things earned salvation; they were demanding them because these were the signs God had given to show who belongs to the people of God and who does not. If the Gentiles believed that they had joined the people of God by faith in Jesus Christ, why would they not want to show this by taking on the marks of God's people? Were they afraid to stand up for their faith?

Dunn supports this view by pointing to the particular phrase that Paul uses of his opponents in Galatians and Romans. Paul categorizes them as being *ex ergon nomou* (lit. 'of works of law'). He is not referring to those who, like the authors of Psalm 19 and 119, seek to obey the law with an attitude of faith, love and gratitude. Rather,

Paul has chosen the phrase to refer to those who are using such laws as 'identity markers' to prevent Gentiles from joining the people of God. With such an understanding, we might paraphrase Paul's response to Peter in Galatians 2.15–16 as follows:

> We ourselves are Jews by birth and not Gentile sinners; yet we know that a person is justified not by possessing the 'identity markers of Judaism' but through faith in Jesus Christ. And we have come to believe in Christ Jesus, so that we might be justified by faith in Christ, and not possession of the 'identity markers of Judaism', because no one will be justified just because they possess the 'identity markers of Judaism'.

This then explains the conclusion to Paul's argument in Galatians 3.6–14, that Christ redeemed us from the curse of the law 'in order that in Christ Jesus the blessing of Abraham might come to the Gentiles' (Gal. 3.14). The problem that Paul is addressing in Galatians is not that no one can keep the law perfectly and so everyone is in need of salvation. It is that the Judaizers' insistence on 'works of law' is preventing God's blessing from coming to the Gentiles. By quoting such texts as Leviticus 18.5 – 'You shall keep my statutes and my ordinances; by doing so one shall live' – they are in fact standing in the way of God's plan to include the Gentiles in the blessing of Abraham. Paul's catchphrase for this is that they are *ex ergon nomou* ('of works of law').

Other New Perspective writers have challenged this understanding of 'works of law' and have developed a range of different ways of explaining the data in Paul's letters.[4] But what unites them is their opposition to what is often referred to as 'the Lutheran view' that imposes on Paul – and Jesus – a fundamental dichotomy between 'believing' and 'doing'. This is often focused on Paul's use of Habakkuk 2.4 (Gal. 3.11; Rom. 1.17) and Leviticus 18.5 (Gal. 3.12; Rom. 10.5). In the Hebrew text of Habakkuk 2.4 the key word is the Hebrew adjective *emunah*. It occurs some 49 times in the Hebrew Bible, frequently referring to God's faithfulness (Deut. 32.4; Ps. 36.5; Isa. 25.1; Lam. 3.23), but also the demand for human faithfulness (Prov. 12.22) or simply 'truth' (Jer. 5.1). Thus the meaning of Habakkuk 2.4 is that despite the calamities that are unfolding, the righteous person is to remain faithful (lit. 'by his faithfulness, he will live'). In other words, it not only assumes an attitude of faith (believing in God's promises), it also involves actions (continuing in the covenant). There is no suggestion that Habakkuk is making a distinction between 'living by faith' and 'living by works'. The two are combined in the concept of faithfulness (see Appendix 3 for the Qumran understanding).

The LXX uses the phrase *ek pisteos* ('out of/from faith') to translate this, and one could argue that this rather unusual expression (only here in the LXX) is thus different from the meaning of the Hebrew. However, the LXX also has a different pronoun, so that the righteous person now lives by God's *pistis*, not their own; the meaning of the LXX is that the righteous person lives by God's faithfulness (hardly God's faith). This certainly involves trusting in God's faithfulness but again, there is no implication that 'works' are excluded. Living by God's faithfulness means living faithfully in the covenant that God has graciously bestowed on Israel; that is, keeping the law.

So unless Paul is substantially changing the meaning of Habakkuk 2.4, Romans 1.17 and Galatians 3.11 are asserting that 'the righteous live by faithfulness'. Of course, Paul now understands 'faithfulness' to include the revelation that 'in Christ God was reconciling the world to himself' (2 Cor. 5.19) and hence, ironically, those who are insisting on the law are in fact opposing God's purposes. But he is not reading into the Habakkuk verse a faith–works dichotomy that is not there. He can now speak more definitively of what sort of faithfulness God requires, but it is not a change from *earning* salvation to *receiving* salvation. The former has never been a possibility in Judaism.

Similarly with Leviticus 18.5. The context is that God is warning the people not to take up the practices of the Canaanites when they enter the promised land. Instead, they are to abide by the covenant; that is, they are to obey God's statutes and ordinances, and in so doing they will live (*zesetai*). This is the same word as in Habakkuk 2.4, where the righteous will live (*zesetai*) by faithfulness. The two verses are not in contradiction, as if one says that life comes through the law and the other that life comes through faith. For those living within God's covenant, faithfulness implies obeying God's statutes and ordinances. Of course, the prophets were constantly reminding Israel of the danger of using external observance as a cover for neglecting the needs of the poor and the outcast. Thus Hosea 6.6 describes God as saying: 'For I desire steadfast love and not sacrifice, the knowledge of God rather than burnt offerings' (quoted in Matt. 9.13 and 12.7). But the book of Hosea as a whole is not calling for the abandonment of law in favour of some sort of 'heart religion'. It is a call for faithfulness, which not only involves loving God and neighbour but also offering the appropriate sacrifices when sin disrupts those relationships.

So when Paul quotes Leviticus 18.5 in Romans 10.5, it is not intended as a contrast to the 'righteousness that comes from faith'. Paul has asserted in Romans 10.4 that Christ is the *telos* of the law. This could mean 'end', but many scholars think 'goal' is the correct translation. Correctly understood, the goal of the law is Christ. In defence of this assertion Paul cites Leviticus 18.5 to the effect that obedience was required to maintain the covenant ('will live'), and then Deuteronomy 30.12–14, which through its mention of heart and lips Paul interprets as a reference to Christ. As Wagner puts it:

> Paul refracts Leviticus 18:5 through the twin lenses of Deuteronomy 30:12–14 and of his gospel 'to the Jew first and also to the Greek' in order to show that God has now acted in Christ to realize the Law's promise of life for all who will respond with heart and mouth to the word that is near.[5]

Indeed, Wagner follows Hays's suggestion that Paul would have found in the final chapters of Deuteronomy a prophetic summary of the gospel. In the so-called 'Song of Moses' in Deuteronomy 32, Paul would have read of God's gracious election of Israel, her preservation in the wilderness and gift of the promised land. He would also have read of Israel's repeated rebellions, the jealous anger of God and the curses that will come upon them. But lastly, he will have read of 'the power and faithfulness of Israel's God, who will arise "at the end of days" to defeat his enemies and to vindicate his people, and whose glory will be celebrated by all creation – the heavens and the angelic beings, the nations together with his people'.[6] And the evidence that Paul has thought long and hard about Deuteronomy 32 can be seen from his explicit quotations: Deuteronomy 32.21 in Romans 10.19; 32.35 in Romans 12.19; and 32.43 in Romans 15.10.

Justification by Christ's faithfulness

If it is correct that in the Habakkuk quotation, *ek pisteos* refers to faithfulness, what is its meaning in texts where justification is said to be *ek pisteos Christou*? The NRSV translates Galatians 2.16 as follows:

> we know that a person is justified not by the works of the law but through faith in Jesus Christ [*dia pisteos Iesou Christou*]. And we have come to believe in Christ Jesus [*eis Christon Iesoun*], so that we might be justified by faith in Christ [*ek pisteos Christou*], and not by doing the works of the law, because no one will be justified by the works of the law.

There is no doubt that the middle expression (*eis Christon Iesoun*) understands Christ as the object of the believing, and so 'believe in Christ' is the correct translation. But do the other two expressions – using different prepositions and the genitive case – mean the same thing (as NRSV), or do they refer to a quality of Christ, namely his faithfulness? In other words, does this verse make two points about justification? The first comes from the middle expression and states the need for believing or trusting in Christ. The second comes from the first and third expressions and states that justification comes 'through' (*dia*) or 'out of' (*ek*) the faithfulness of Christ. It is not referring to a human quality (faith) but Christ's faithfulness in fulfilling his mission.

On Greek grammar

Greek is what is called an inflected language; that is, the spelling of the noun, known as its 'case', changes depending on whether it is the subject ('*cat* chases dog' – known as the nominative) or object ('dog chases *cat*' – known as the accusative). Meaning is not determined by word order, as in English, but by the 'case' of the noun. There are three other cases: vocative, genitive and dative. The vocative is used for direct address (*kyrie* is the vocative form of *kyrios*, as in *kyrie eleison*, 'Lord, have mercy'). The genitive (*kyriou*) is most often used for possession ('of the Lord') or separation ('from the Lord') but can also indicate other relationships ('with respect to the Lord'). The dative (*kyrio*) is used for the indirect object of a sentence ('to the Lord' or 'for the Lord') or the instrument ('by the Lord') or accompaniment ('with the Lord'). In order to distinguish which usage is intended, prepositions (words like 'in', 'out', 'upon', 'towards') are used. The difficulty is that unlike English, Greek prepositions do not have a fixed meaning but derive their meaning from the case of the noun and the particular context. Hence the problem in deciding whether the three phrases in Galatians 2.16 refer to the same thing ('faith in Christ') or are purposely different.

Krister Stendahl (1976) argued that Romans is not so much about how human beings can be saved (justification by faith) but rather is a defence of God's faithfulness. Hays (1983) builds on this by arguing that Paul's doctrine of justification revolves around faithfulness, namely Christ's faithfulness in life and death.[7] He supports this by pointing to Romans 5, where Adam's act of disobedience leads to condemnation but Christ's act of obedience leads to justification. Of course, it is crucial for Paul that people confess with their lips and believe in their hearts (Rom. 10.9), but the emphasis is on what Christ has done, not human faith. Indeed, Hays thinks that Paul has understood the Habakkuk quotation in Romans 1.17 as messianic – '*The righteous one* will live by faithfulness' – rather than as a reference to believers. He cites the opening of Romans, where Paul states that Jesus Christ was 'promised beforehand through his prophets in the holy scriptures' (Rom. 1.2), and deduces that Paul's first explicit quotation in Romans is likely to be about Christ rather than believers. Few have followed him in this, but many have been persuaded by his view that justification derives from 'the faithfulness of Christ'.[8]

Not the New Perspective

Francis Watson agrees with the New Perspective that it was a grave error to caricature all forms of Judaism as 'legalistic' or 'works religion'. This is not only offensive but also academically lazy, as if one word or phrase can adequately capture the complexity of a living religion. However, he thinks the New Perspective has fallen into the same trap when it labels all forms of Judaism (and Paul) as 'covenantal nomism' (grace followed by obedience). This umbrella term fails to notice the very real differences that exist between Paul and the various forms of Judaism that existed in his day, as well as the different strands of thought that can be found in Scripture itself. He thus draws attention to Galatians 3.11–12, where Paul is quite clearly contrasting Leviticus 18.5 with Habakkuk 2.4:

Now it is evident that no one is justified before God by the law; for 'The one who is righteous will live by faith [*ek pisteos*].' But the law does not rest on faith [*ek pisteos*]; on the contrary, 'Whoever does the works of the law will live by them.'

Although there are disputes about the meaning of Habakkuk 2.4 and Leviticus 18.5, there is no doubt that Paul has inserted the comment between them (lit. 'But the law is not of faith'). The use of the same expression (*ek pisteos*) that occurs in Habakkuk 2.4 confirms that Paul is intending a contrast, and the quotation that follows (Lev. 18.5) forms the substance of that contrast. Leviticus 18.5 promises life through the law, and this is in contrast to Habakkuk 2.4, which promises life through faith/fulness. Thus the debate as to whether Habakkuk 2.4 means faith or faithfulness is not really the issue. The point is that Paul is drawing attention to two texts from Scripture that promise life, and asserting that they are opposed to one another. Watson's word for this is 'antithesis'. So Paul begins his argument in Galatians 3 with the quotation of Genesis 15.6 ('Abraham believed God and it was reckoned to him as righteousness') and pairs this with Habakkuk 2.4 ('The righteous by faith will live'). But in contrast to such unconditional promises, Scripture also knows of another set of promises, which are conditional in nature. Leviticus 18.5 stands as a representative of all such texts that promise life – or blessing – *on condition* of obedience to the law.

Watson's major thesis is that Paul read the Pentateuch as a whole and deduced that it both offers life through obedience to the law and states that such obedience is impossible. This can be seen in Deuteronomy 27—28. Deuteronomy 27 consists of a list of curses that will come upon Israel if they forsake God's law, while Deuteronomy 28 opens with the promise of blessing if they keep it: '*If* you will only obey the LORD your God, by diligently observing all his commandments that I am commanding you today…all these blessings shall come upon you and overtake you, *if* you obey the LORD your God.' It therefore appears that curse and blessing are real possibilities, but as we read on it becomes clear that curse is the inevitable result of such an offer: 'All these curses *shall come upon you*, pursuing and overtaking you until you are destroyed, *because you did not obey the* LORD *your God*, by observing the commandments and the decrees that he commanded you' (Deut. 28.45).

Modern scholars recognize this as a reference to the exile, and written by those who witnessed it. Deuteronomy is not a unified book written by Moses but a collection of traditions, some of which date from a much later time. But Paul would have read it as a prophecy that though blessing through obedience to the law is a genuine offer, it will in fact lead to curse. Most Jews of Paul's day drew the conclusion that they must avoid a repetition of the exile generation by a renewed commitment to the law. Indeed, that is precisely what Deuteronomy 30 urges. But Paul drew the conclusion that it points to another way, namely the unconditional promise made to Abraham (Gen. 15.6) and the succinct statement of it in Habakkuk 2.4. Paul makes this clear in his analogy of a human will or testament, which does not change its 'promise' character if codicils are later added:

> Brothers and sisters, I give an example from daily life: once a person's will has been ratified, no one adds to it or annuls it. Now the promises were made to Abraham and to his offspring; it does not say, 'And to offsprings', as of many; but it says, 'And to your offspring', that is, to one person, who is Christ. My point is this: the law, which came four hundred and thirty years later, does not annul a covenant previously ratified by God, so as to nullify the promise. For if the inheritance comes from the law, it no longer comes from the promise; but God granted it to Abraham through the promise.
>
> (Gal. 3.15–18)

Thus Scripture does not speak with one voice, and Paul has recognized this. His opponents are trying to force it to speak with one voice (the righteous must live by faithfulness to the law, even if their righteousness comes from faith in Christ), as are the proponents of the New Perspective (all is 'covenantal nomism'). But Paul has seen what they have not seen, namely that Scripture is divided against itself. This is also Watson's explanation for why Paul can quote a text like Leviticus 18.5 ('Whoever does the works of the law will live by them') for its negative witness, while quoting Leviticus 19.18 ('You shall love your neighbour as yourself') as God's will for the Christian community. As Watson says:

> the text that derives from the Sinai event is multiple and not singular in its origin (cf. Gal. 3.19–20). From one angelic voice we learn that the person who does these things will live by them; from another we

learn that all who are of works of law are under a curse; a third instructs
us to love our neighbour as ourselves; a fourth is concerned with the
observance of sacred times and seasons (cf. Gal. 4.9–10).[9]

Some would conclude from this that Paul's use of Scripture is
arbitrary, picking and choosing what he accepts or rejects, but Watson
denies this. He thinks that these 'voices' are not being *imposed*
on Scripture but are really present. Paul can be said to be a faithful
interpreter of Scripture because he is following the contours of
Scripture itself.

Paul has a developing/contradictory view of the law

Hans Hübner is particularly associated with the opinion that Paul's
view of the law underwent a transformation between the writing
of Galatians and Romans. In Galatians, Paul is still stinging from
what he perceives as a betrayal of the gospel (Gal. 1.6) and of him
(Gal. 4.19). He is not interested in offering a mediating position
that recognizes that some aspects of the law are good. He wishes to
prise them away from the Judaizers by discrediting the law as a
means of righteousness, hence his statements are uncompromising:
'You are observing special days, and months, and seasons, and
years. I am afraid that my work for you may have been wasted'
(Gal. 4.10–11).

But Romans is a different situation altogether. Paul has never
visited Rome (Rom. 1.13) and cannot be sure what they think of him
(Rom. 3.8). His tone is conciliatory and his statements are therefore
more balanced. We have the same rejection of the law as a means of
righteousness (Rom. 3.20), but also positive statements like Romans
3.31 ('Do we then overthrow the law by this faith? By no means!
On the contrary, we uphold the law') and Romans 7.12 ('So the law
is holy, and the commandment is holy and just and good'). In
Hübner's view, Romans represents Paul's more considered and mature
view of the law.[10]

In contrast, the Finnish scholar Heikki Räisänen has championed
the assertion that Paul's view of the law is utterly contradictory. He
rejects Hübner's attempt to explain the differences as a development
from Galatians to Romans by pointing out that the differences are
present in both letters. Thus Galatians does have positive statements
about the law, as when Paul quotes Leviticus 19.18 – 'Love your

neighbour as yourself' – in Galatians 5.14 and urges his readers/ hearers to 'fulfil the law of Christ' in Galatians 6.2. And in Romans, the positive statements about the law in Romans 7.12, 14 are simply incompatible with his marriage analogy in Romans 7.1–4 and his deduction in Romans 7.6 that 'we have been released from the law so that we serve in the new way of the Spirit, and not in the old way of the written code'.[11]

Conclusion

Given the conflicting opinions concerning Paul's view of the law, one might conclude that Räisänen is correct: Paul's statements cannot be reconciled into a single coherent view. However, many scholars regard this as an abdication and therefore continue to search for an overall perspective that will make sense of his many statements about the law. Watson has presented one of the most comprehensive views to date, but its strength might also be its weakness. If the explanation of any particular use of Scripture is that Paul heard this as a positive voice or heard it as a negative voice, are we really dealing with an explanation? It surely implies another question: What was it that led Paul to reckon some verses as the positive voice and others as the negative voice? The New Perspective marks a turning point in Pauline studies, not least for exposing the lazy caricatures of Jewish beliefs in the first century. It has shown that 'faithfulness' is something God required of the Jews and continues to require of Christians. However, against the New Perspective, some maintain that this parallel, true as it is, does not get to the heart of the matter. Righteousness by the law and righteousness by faith are two quite different pathways and are key to understanding Paul.[12]

5

Paul and the prophets:
Israel and the Gentiles

Introduction

There are about 32 explicit quotations from the prophets in Paul's undisputed letters (see Appendix 2), of which the majority come from the book of Isaiah (23). No wonder the subtitle of Ross Wagner's book, *Heralds of the Good News*, is *Isaiah and Paul 'In Concert' in the Letter to the Romans*.[1] Thirteen of the Isaiah quotations are taken from the first half of the book (chs 1, 8, 10, 11, 22, 25, 27, 28, 29) and ten from the second half (chs 40, 49, 52, 53, 54, 59, 64, 65). It is of interest that although there are six explicit quotations from Isaiah 52—54, none of them are used to explain the meaning of Christ's death as 'the suffering servant'. The only quotation from Isaiah 53 (Rom. 10.16) is from the first verse – 'Who has believed what we have heard?' – and refers to Jewish unbelief.[2] Indeed, very few of the quotations from the prophets are applied directly to Christ. Instead, Paul applies them to the proclamation of the gospel, the inclusion of the Gentiles, the current unbelief of the Jews, future salvation and the life of the Church.

There are three quotations from the book of Hosea, which are applied to the inclusion of the Gentiles (Hos. 1.10; 2.23 in Romans 9.25–26) and Christ's victory over death (Hos. 13.14 in 1 Cor. 15.55). Each of them is closely co-ordinated with quotations from Isaiah, and it may be that they came to mind because of similarities of thought and vocabulary. There is only one quotation from the book of Habakkuk (2.4), but as we have already noted, its importance for Paul is demonstrated by its pivotal place in the argument of Galatians 3.6–14 and the fact that it is the opening quotation in Romans (1.17). Although it only consists of six words (lit. 'the righteous by faith will live'), it has had an enormous influence on the interpretation of Paul.

There is a quotation from Jeremiah 9.24 ('Let the one who boasts, boast in the LORD') in 1 Corinthians 1.31 and 2 Corinthians 10.17, and a quotation from Ezekiel 37.27 ('I will be their God, and they shall be my people') in 2 Corinthians 6.16. The following verse (2 Cor. 6.17) is a quotation from Isaiah 52.11, but the phrase 'then I will welcome you' is probably an allusion to Ezekiel 20.34, 41. In Romans 10.13, Joel 2.32 – 'Everyone who calls on the name of the LORD shall be saved' – is quoted, and since Paul sees Jesus as Lord (*kyrios*) it is easy to see why this verse appealed to him. Finally, there is a brief quotation from Malachi 1.2–3 ('I have loved Jacob, but I have hated Esau'), already discussed in Chapter 3 (see p. 49). In this chapter we will discuss Paul's use of the prophets under the first four themes mentioned above: the proclamation of the gospel; the inclusion of the Gentiles; the current unbelief of the Jews; future salvation. In the next chapter we will consider how Paul uses the prophets to speak to current issues in the Church and the behaviour of Christians.

The proclamation of the gospel

In Romans 10.1, Paul speaks again (cf. Rom. 9.1–5) of his heartfelt desire to see his own people find salvation in Christ. He applies Deuteronomy 30.14 – 'The word is near you, on your lips and in your heart' – to the gospel, which he summarizes in two statements: 'if you *confess* with your lips that Jesus is Lord and *believe* in your heart that God raised him from the dead, you will be saved' (Rom. 10.9). Paul is no doubt quoting an early Christian creed, but the language – believe, saved, Lord – allows him to draw on a number of scriptural texts in support. The first is the second half of Isaiah 28.16 (lit. 'Every one who believes in him will not be put to shame'). Paul has already quoted this text in Romans 9.33, where the emphasis fell on the first part of the verse, that unbelieving Jews have stumbled over the stone that God has laid in Zion (see below, p. 81). For the second half of the verse, the original text – Greek and Hebrew – refers more generally to 'the one who believes', and this is how Paul quotes it in Romans 9.33. But in Romans 10.11, he adds the word *pas* ('all') to highlight the universal nature of the gospel (lit. 'every one who believes').[3]

His explanatory comment in Romans 10.12 – 'For there is no distinction between Jew and Greek; the same Lord is Lord of *all* and is generous to *all* who call on him' – emphasizes the *all*, while offering an equivalent to 'believing in him', namely 'calling on him'. This is in preparation for the quotation from Joel 2.32, which says: 'Everyone (*pas*) who calls on the name of the Lord shall be saved' (Rom. 10.13). The use of *saved* now connects with the early Christian creed that those who confess that Jesus is Lord and believe that God raised him from the dead will be *saved*. Of course, the word *saved* would have been understood differently in Joel's day. Indeed, if we read on from Joel 2.32 we find that the promise is not quite as universal as it sounds, for it refers specifically to the 'fortunes of Judah and Jerusalem' whereas the nations will face judgement (Joel 3).

It is worth noting that many scholars also see an allusion to Joel 2.32 in Paul's introduction to 1 Corinthians, where he expands the reference to the church in Corinth with the words, 'together with *all those who* in every place *call on the name of our Lord* Jesus Christ, both their Lord and ours' (1 Cor. 1.2). Since Paul follows this with mention of enriched speech (v. 5), spiritual gifts (v. 7a) and the 'day of our Lord' (v. 7b), all key themes in Joel, the allusion is very probable. In this verse the universal meaning is heightened by the addition 'in every place', perhaps a deliberate expansion of Joel's limitation to Judah and Jerusalem. If Paul thinks his readers – or some of them – would know the Joel text and thus spot his additions, it may be that he is trying to convey the view that in the light of the Christ-event, the semantic potential of Joel 2.32 has finally been realized; he said more than he knew.

In Romans 10.14–21, Paul continues to probe the Scriptures for an explanation of why many Jews have not 'called on the name of the Lord'. We will discuss the negative side of this below, but there is one thing he is clear about: the gospel has been proclaimed. This is summarized in a quotation of Psalm 19.4 in Romans 10.18 ('Their voice has gone out to all the earth, and their words to the ends of the world'), but before that he cites Isaiah 52.7 in the form: 'How beautiful are the feet of those who bring good news' (Rom. 10.15). In Isaiah the reference is to a single herald ('How beautiful upon the mountains are the feet *of the messenger* who announces peace, who brings good news'), but since the scope of the good news is that 'all the ends of the earth shall see the salvation of God' (Isa. 52.10), logic demands that it must refer to a plurality of heralds.[4] And Paul connects this plurality with those, like him, commissioned to preach the gospel. That Paul sees himself as part of this fulfilment is confirmed in Romans 15.21, where he states that his ambition is to preach the gospel in places where it has not been preached, and cites Isaiah 52.15 in support: 'Those who have never been told of him shall see, and those who have never heard of him shall understand.' Thus Paul is not only supporting his claim that the proclamation of the gospel is prefigured in Scripture; he also thinks that Scripture speaks of his own commission to preach to those who have not yet had the opportunity to respond to it.

The inclusion of the Gentiles

Paul's argument for the inclusion of the Gentiles in Galatians 3—4 and Romans 4, where the pressing issue is whether Gentile believers need to submit to circumcision, revolves around the figure of Abraham. Since Abraham 'believed God' (Gen. 15) *and* submitted to circumcision (Gen. 17), it is easy to see how Paul's opponents thought that Gentile Christians should do likewise. In Romans 9—11, Paul argues on a broader canvas, that it has always been God's plan to include Gentiles. But unlike the traditional Jewish idea that God would first restore Zion and then Gentiles would join them (the so-called 'pilgrimage of the nations' – see Isaiah 2.2–4), Paul argues that Israel's present unbelief will continue until 'the full number of the Gentiles has come in' (Rom. 11.25), and then Israel/Zion will be restored (Rom. 11.26). Paul looks primarily to Hosea and Isaiah in order to support this reversal of Jewish eschatology.

In Romans 9.22–23, Paul asks two hypothetical questions as an illustration that a pot (human being) has no right to question the potter (God) as to why he chooses to make different objects from the same batch of clay: '*What if* God, desiring to show his wrath and to make known his power, endured with much patience the objects of wrath that are made for destruction; and *what if* he has done so in order to make known the riches of his glory for the objects of mercy, which he has prepared beforehand for glory –'. The questions go unanswered (indicated by the dash in the NRSV), but he explains that the 'objects of mercy' include 'us whom he has called, not from the Jews only but also from the Gentiles' (Rom. 9.24). This is then supported by a composite quotation of Hosea 2.23 and 1.10:

Those who were not my people I will call 'my people', and her who was not beloved I will call 'beloved'. And in the very place where it was said to them, 'You are not my people', there they shall be called children of the living God.

(Rom. 9.25–26)

In the form that Paul quotes them, both quotations assert that those who were previously outside God's promises ('not my people/ not beloved') have become God's people ('my people/beloved/ children of the living God'). Since it is clear that Paul believes the Jews are God's people (Rom. 9.4–5) and that Jacob/Israel is the one loved (Rom. 9.13), he appears to be applying the Hosea texts to Gentiles, or at least to the inclusion of Gentiles into those who 'shall be called children of the living God'. The only issue that might puzzle his readers is the reference to 'in the very place it was said to them'. To what could this possibly refer? In search of an answer they would perhaps seek further insight from the book of Hosea, where they would discover two things. First, Paul talks about a reversal for 'not my people' and 'not beloved', whereas Hosea 2.23 speaks of 'not shown mercy' and 'not my people'. Interestingly, Hosea 2.23 is also quoted in 1 Peter 2.10, where 'not shown mercy' is retained, but like Paul, the 'not my people' clause comes first: 'Once you were not a people, but now you are God's people; once you had not received mercy, but now you have received mercy.' It is possible that the Hosea text existed in a variety of forms in the first century.

Second, the context of the quotations in Hosea shows that it is disobedient Israel who are the 'not shown mercy/not my people' and, correspondingly, to whom the promise of restoration refers. Thus the clause, 'in the very place where it was said to them, "You are not my people"', is a reference to Northern Israel, and the hope expressed is that the 'people of Judah and the people of Israel shall be gathered together' (Hos. 1.11). How then does Paul think these texts support the inclusion of the Gentiles? The simplest answer is that when Israel was called 'not my people' they had – temporarily – become like Gentiles. So when Hosea says that God will make 'not my people' into 'my people', Paul draws the conclusion that it not only applies to rebellious Jews but to Gentiles, who have always been regarded as 'not my people'.

Alternatively, it could be argued that Paul is not intending the Hosea quotations to support the statement in Romans 9.24 ('not from the Jews only but also from the Gentiles') but the statement in Romans 9.23 ('to make known the riches of his glory for the objects of mercy'). The two quotations from Hosea are then illustrations of God's mercy in the past rather than specific references to Gentile inclusion. If this is the case, then the next verse, 'And Isaiah cries out concerning Israel', does not represent a change of subject – Israel rather than Gentiles – but qualifies the promise of 'not my people' becoming 'my people' by referring to the remnant; it does not – currently – apply to all Israel. However, after the two Isaiah quotations (Rom. 9.27–29) Paul draws the conclusion that 'Gentiles, who did not strive for righteousness, have attained it', while 'Israel, who did strive for the righteousness that is based on law, did not succeed in fulfilling that law' (Rom. 9.30–31). It does therefore seem that Paul is applying the Hosea quotations to support the inclusion of the Gentiles, even though this was not the original meaning in Hosea. The (surprising) success of the Gentile mission has given Paul a unique insight into how the scriptural promises are to be fulfilled, and hence a reconfiguration of their meaning. As Hays poetically puts it, it is 'as though the light of the gospel shining through the text has illuminated a latent sense so brilliant that the opaque original sense has vanished altogether'.[5]

A similar issue faces us when we try to understand Romans 10.19–21. Paul begins with a quotation from Deuteronomy 32.21 that speaks of making Israel jealous by 'those who are not a nation'. He ends with a quotation from Isaiah 65.2 in the form, 'All day long I have held out my hands to a disobedient and contrary people', and he underlines the point that it is a reference to Israel: 'But of Israel he says.' In between, Paul quotes Isaiah 65.1 in the form, 'I have been found by those who did not seek me; I have shown myself to those who did not ask for me.' In Isaiah it is clear that Isaiah 65.1 and 65.2 are referring to the same subject (rebellious Israel), but Paul's introduction to Isaiah 65.2 (*'But* of Israel') suggests a change of subject, as if Isaiah 65.1 was speaking about the 'not a nation' referred to in Deuteronomy 32.21, namely the Gentiles. Thus Paul drives a wedge between Isaiah 65.1 and 65.2, applying the first sentence to Gentiles responding to God's overtures ('I have been found') and the second to Israel's stubborn refusal:

Again I ask, did Israel not understand? First Moses says, 'I will make you jealous of those who are *not a nation*; with a foolish nation I will make you angry.' Then Isaiah is so ,bold as to say, 'I have been found by those who *did not seek me*; I have shown myself to those who *did not ask for me.*' But of Israel he says, 'All day long I have held out my hands to a disobedient and contrary people.'

(Rom. 10.19–21)

Though there is no grammatical doubt that Isaiah 65.1 and 65.2 refer to the same subject, there are two things that might have acted as a catalyst for Paul's innovative interpretation. The first is that Isaiah 65.1 speaks about a '*nation* that did not call on my name' (though Paul does not quote this part of the text), whereas Isaiah 65.2 speaks of God holding out his hands to a 'rebellious *people*'. In the original, both of these terms refer to Israel, but Paul never uses 'nation' (*ethnos*) to speak about Israel; it is his word – usually in the plural – for 'Gentiles'. Second, there is some tension between the content of the two verses. Isaiah 65.1 states that God has been found by those who did not seek him, but Isaiah 65.2 says that God has held out his hands to a rebellious people. This is eased in the NRSV to 'I was *ready to be found* by those who did not ask', implying that it did not in fact happen. But the Hebrew and Greek are statements of fact ('I was found'), which presumably must be taken as ironic. So although Paul has found a reference to Gentile inclusion in a text that did not originally refer to Gentiles (as with Hosea), we can perhaps see glimpses of how he was able to do this; the two verses sit somewhat uncomfortably together. As Wagner observes, it is part of an interpretative strategy where Paul finds references to Gentiles in 'negatively phrased descriptions of people (often Israelites!) who are estranged from God'.[6]

As Paul draws his letter to the Romans to a close, he quotes a series of texts that all contain the word 'Gentiles'. It is probably significant that these are taken from the three divisions of the Hebrew Scriptures: law (Deut. 32.43); prophets (Isa. 11.10); and writings (Ps. 18.49; 117.1). But it is only Isaiah who is specifically named, and his text seems to be the most theologically significant:

For I tell you that Christ has become a servant of the circumcised on behalf of the truth of God in order that he might confirm the promises given to the patriarchs, and in order that the *Gentiles* might glorify God for his mercy. As it is written, 'Therefore I will confess you

79

among the *Gentiles*, and sing praises to your name'; and again he
says, 'Rejoice, O *Gentiles*, with his people'; and again, 'Praise the Lord,
all you *Gentiles*, and let all the peoples praise him'; and again Isaiah
says, 'The root of Jesse shall come, the one who rises to rule the *Gentiles*;
in him the *Gentiles* shall hope.'

(Rom. 15.8–12)

The messianic prophecy of Isaiah 11 speaks of a new exodus for Israel
('so there shall be a highway from Assyria for the remnant that is left
of his people, as there was for Israel when they came up from the
land of Egypt' – v. 16), which will be a 'sign' or 'signal' for the peoples/
nations (Isa. 11.10, 12). The immediate context suggests a negative
meaning for 'sign' (portent?), though verse 10 ('the nations shall
inquire of him') is suggestive of something more positive. This is
made explicit in the LXX, which says, 'the nations shall *hope* in him',
aided perhaps by the positive statements that follow in Isaiah 12.3,
5. This is the form in which Paul quotes Isaiah 11.10 in Romans
15.12, bringing his argument for the inclusion of the Gentiles to a
close. It is interesting that although Paul clearly sees Jesus as the
fulfilment of the 'root of Jesse' promise, that is not why he is quoting
it here. As Wagner says: 'Paul's main concern in Romans 15:12 is not
to "prove" something about Jesus, but to show that scripture prophesies the inclusion of Gentiles in the worshipping community as a
result of what God has done in and through Jesus Christ.'[7] But as we
have seen, he can only do this by subjecting the text to some fairly
significant interpretative changes.

The current unbelief of the Jews

If the theme of Gentile inclusion requires explanation and scriptural
support, then so does the theme of Israel's current unbelief. In Romans
2.17–29, Paul castigates Jewish teachers who claim to be a 'light to
those who are in darkness' (Rom. 2.19) but are guilty of theft,
adultery and robbing temples (Rom. 2.22). It is difficult to imagine
that Paul thinks this is literally true of all teachers, and perhaps he
is thinking of the inner attitudes that lead to such crimes, as in the
Sermon on the Mount. The indictment is provided by a quotation
from Isaiah 52.5, in which the LXX can be understood as saying:
'The name of God is blasphemed among the Gentiles *because of you.*'
The Hebrew text does not speak of Gentiles or indeed of blame;
it is more the piteous state of Israel – 'my people are taken away

80

without cause' – that has led to God's name being despised, presumably because outsiders will conclude that he cannot be much of a god if he is not even able to protect his own people. Paul's use of the text as an accusation not only depends on the LXX's reference to 'among the Gentiles', but a particular interpretation of its other addition (*di' humas*), which Paul takes as 'because of your fault' rather than the more general 'concerning you'.[8]

In Romans 3.2–3 the image moves from breaking the law to the sin of unbelief. Utilizing a play on words, Paul says in Romans 3.2 that the Jews were 'entrusted' (*pisteuo*) with the oracles of God, and then asks in Romans 3.3: 'What if some were unfaithful (*apisteo*)? Will their unfaithfulness (*apistia*) nullify the faithfulness (*pistis*) of God?' The idea is instantly dismissed, and Paul quotes 'So that you may be justified in your words, and prevail in your judging' (based on Psalm 51.4) to show that God's word can never be nullified. The issue is then taken up again in Romans 9—11. We have already seen how Paul contrasts the reversals of Hosea 1.10; 2.23 ('not my people'/'my people') with a quotation concerning Israel (Rom. 9.27). In fact two quotations follow, both with the idea of God's promises being realized through a remnant.[9] The positive aspects of this are taken up in Romans 11, but here Paul talks about Israel stumbling over the stumbling stone, which he supports with a quotation of Isaiah 28.16, with a phrase – 'a rock that will make them fall' – from Isaiah 8.14:

See, I am laying in Zion a stone that will make people stumble, a rock that will make them fall, *and whoever believes in him will not be put to shame.*

(Rom. 9.33)

See, I am laying in Zion a foundation *stone*, a tested stone, a precious cornerstone, a sure foundation: *'One who trusts will not panic.'*

(Isa. 28.16)

He will become a sanctuary, a *stone* one strikes against; for both houses of Israel he will become a rock one *stumbles over* – a trap and a snare for the inhabitants of Jerusalem.

(Isa. 8.14)

It is easy to see how these two 'stone' texts might have come together in Paul's mind, but it is interesting that they are also both quoted in

1 Peter 2.6–8 (separately), along with the 'cornerstone' text from Psalm 118.22 (also quoted in the Gospels). It looks as though the early Church was particularly interested in these 'stone' texts as an explanation for belief and unbelief. Paul will apply the final clause (LXX: lit. 'the one who believes in it/him will not be ashamed') to Christians who confess Jesus as Lord, but the point here is that Israel has stumbled over the stumbling stone through unbelief, and will thus be put to shame.

Testimony hypothesis

What is interesting about the quotations of Isaiah 8.14 and 28.16 in Romans and 1 Peter is that instead of the LXX's verb for 'I am laying' (*embalo*), they both use the verb *tithemi* ('I put'), and instead of the LXX's phrase for 'rock of falling' (*petras ptomati*), they both use *petra(n) skandalou* ('rock of stumbling'). It is inconceivable that both decided to change the wording of the LXX and happened to agree, and so some form of literary dependence is required. Since most scholars find it unlikely that either knew the other's work, Rendel Harris (1920) developed the theory that both are quoting from a collection of testimonies that were compiled to aid Christians in their debates with the Jews. This explains why the wording sometimes differs from the texts that have come down to us, and why the texts are sometimes taken out of context. Building on this, Charles Dodd (1952) put forward the theory that the New Testament authors were not quoting a 'testimony book' but blocks of Scripture that were related by theme (e.g. the servant passages in Isaiah, the apocalyptic passages in Joel 2—3, Zechariah 9—14, Daniel 7). He thus denied that texts were taken out of context; they were in context if one considered the block of material from which they were taken. Other suggestions were that the combination of passages derive from the liturgical life of the Church or indeed are excerpts from early Christian hymns. The discovery of hymn collections, excerpted texts and testimony collections among the Dead Sea Scrolls (see Appendix 3) has kept this a live debate.[10]

Since Paul's vocation was to travel the world and preach to Gentiles, he might have been sensitive to the criticism that he had not done much to bring the gospel to his fellow Jews. That might explain his insistence that the message of the gospel has gone out to the 'ends of the earth', which he supports with quotations from Isaiah 53.1 and Psalm 19.4 (Rom. 10.18). Isaiah 53.1 reinforces his point that it is unbelief that is causing Israel to stumble, but he introduces the quotation with the words, 'But not all have obeyed the good news'. For Paul, the gospel has been proclaimed and heard, so that unbelief is disobedience, the refusal to believe. It is captured in his quotation of Isaiah 65.2, that God has held out his hands to a disobedient and contrary people 'all day long'. But Paul will not allow the destiny of anyone to depend on their own choices and actions. Israel's failure to obtain what it was seeking is ultimately part of God's plan. So just as Isaiah says that God has caused a 'sluggish spirit' to come over Israel's prophets (Isa. 29.10), and Moses tells the wilderness generation that God has not given them eyes to see or ears to hear 'down to this day' (Deut. 29.4), Paul now produces a composite quotation to apply to unbelieving Israel: 'God gave them a sluggish spirit, eyes that would not see and ears that would not hear, down to this very day' (Rom. 11.8). As Paul reads Scripture, Moses and Isaiah are both witnesses to Israel's current unbelief.

Future salvation

As noted above, Paul says in Romans 3.3 that the unfaithfulness of *some* Jews will not nullify the faithfulness of God, and he envisages in Romans 9.24 that the 'objects of mercy' consist of Jews and Gentiles. There is debate as to whether the two Isaiah quotations in Romans 9.27–29 emphasize that 'only' a remnant will be saved, or stress that there definitely will be a remnant that is saved. Paul deals with this issue in Romans 11. He begins by asking the rhetorical question, 'have they stumbled so as to fall?', which he vehemently denies, 'By no means!' (Rom. 11.11). He then explains that Israel's current unbelief has allowed salvation to come to the Gentiles. In a somewhat strained metaphor Paul likens Israel to an olive tree that has had branches cut off to allow for 'wild olive' branches to be grafted in. But if God can accomplish this, he can certainly graft back the natural branches: 'And even those of Israel, if they do not persist in unbelief, will be grafted in, for God has the power to graft them in again' (Rom. 11.23). At this point, it is not clear if God is going to do this, but Paul makes it explicit with a quotation from Isaiah, preceded by a word of explanation:

> I want you to understand this mystery: a hardening has come upon part of Israel, until the full number of the Gentiles has come in. And so all Israel will be saved; as it is written, 'Out of Zion will come the Deliverer; he will banish ungodliness from Jacob.' 'And this is my covenant with them, when I take away their sins.'
>
> (Rom. 11.25b–27)

The claim that 'all Israel will be saved' has perplexed commentators, for Paul has previously contrasted the 'remnant' or 'elect' – as he calls them in Romans 11.7 – with those who lack faith. We have already noted that universalism plays a part in the Adam typology: 'just as one man's trespass led to condemnation for all, so one man's act of righteousness leads to justification and life for all'. Paul now explains the 'mystery' of God's plan: 'God has imprisoned all to disobedience so that he may be merciful to all' (Rom. 11.32). Jews would readily accept that if God were to save Gentiles, it would be through an act of mercy. What Paul has now demonstrated is that Israel is in exactly the same position, and will also receive salvation through God's mercy.

The quotation is taken from Isaiah 59.20, ending with a phrase from Isaiah 27.9. It confirms Paul's confidence that God's promises to Israel have not failed. Isaiah says that a deliverer will come to Zion and banish ungodliness from Jacob/Israel. It is unclear whether Paul is identifying the deliverer with Christ and claiming that ungodliness *has* been banished from Israel. Given the present unbelief of many Jews, it may be that Paul wishes to retain the future tense: there will come a time when God – or perhaps Christ – will banish ungodliness from Israel, and then 'all Israel will be saved'. On the other hand, the phrase taken from Isaiah 29.9 – 'when I take away their sins' – is precisely what Christ is said to have achieved on the cross (Rom. 8.4).

Conclusion

Paul is certain that God's promises to Israel will be fulfilled. Indeed, he believes that the events that have taken place in his lifetime have confirmed that God's plan is being realized, and like other Jews he may have expected a conversion of the Gentiles to follow. What has been surprising for Paul is that many of his fellow Jews have failed to believe, while many of the Gentiles have responded. This has not only caused Paul to rethink the sequence of events predicted by Scripture; it has also given him a hermeneutical perspective to read texts in the light of new revelation. We have seen at least three of these: First, Paul finds references to Gentiles in texts that spoke about the restoration of rebellious Jews who had become 'not my people'; second, Paul finds references to Israel's current unbelief in texts that spoke about Israel's former unbelief; and third, Paul finds references to the salvation of Jews – and Gentiles – in texts that spoke about the restoration of Israel. It is not going too far to call this a 'radical' interpretation but one that is nevertheless thoroughly grounded in Scripture. Speaking of Romans 9—11 in particular, Wagner says: 'Paul has composed this masterpiece out of his own agonized wrestling with the question of God's faithfulness to Israel – a question raised, ironically enough, by his own successful mission to the Gentiles.'[11]

6

Paul and the prophets: the life of the Christian community

Introduction

As well as providing Paul with insights into God's merciful plan for the world, the prophets also help him discern the pattern of life God expects of the Christian community. This is most clearly seen in the Corinthian letters, where the focus is rather more on practical living than the intricate doctrinal debates of Romans and Galatians. We can see this in the way Paul begins to respond to the Corinthians' questions in 1 Corinthians 7.1: 'Now concerning the matters about which you wrote'. He then addresses issues of marriage (1 Cor. 7), food offered to idols (1 Cor. 8—10), worship (1 Cor. 11), spiritual gifts (1 Cor. 12—14), resurrection (1 Cor. 15) and Christian giving (1 Cor. 16). As we have already seen, Paul sees the Christian life as fundamentally rooted in faith (Hab. 2.4 in Rom. 1.17 and Gal. 3.11), which dispels any notion of boasting before God (Rom. 3.27; 4.2). 'Do not let the wise boast in their wisdom...but let those who boast boast in this, that they understand and know me' (Jer. 9.24) is not quoted in Romans or Galatians but occurs twice in the Corinthian letters (1 Cor. 1.31; 2 Cor. 10.17) as 'Let the one who boasts, boast in the Lord'. Human wisdom regards the cross of Christ as foolishness but God thwarts the wisdom of this world (Isa. 29.14) and chooses to reveal it to those who were not expecting it (Isa. 64.4).

Purity and separation are important themes in the Corinthian letters. In 1 Corinthians 5—6, Paul exhorts the Corinthian community to avoid certain kinds of immorality by stating that they are the temple of the Holy Spirit and should be making pure not corrupt offerings to God. In 2 Corinthians 6 he speaks of the Church as the temple of the living God and quotes texts like Isaiah 52.11 – 'Touch no unclean thing; go out from the midst of it; purify yourselves' – to urge separation from evil and evildoers. By identifying the Church with the sacred symbols of Israel's history, Paul evokes the connotations of purity and separation that are associated with them, even while denying their literal ongoing significance.

As 1 Corinthians reaches its climax, Paul offers the ultimate motivation for remaining 'steadfast, immovable, always excelling in the work of the Lord' (1 Cor. 15.58): Christ has defeated death, the ultimate enemy, through his resurrection. Paul supports this through a combined quotation of Isaiah 25.8 and Hosea 13.14, which he quotes in the form: 'Death has been swallowed up in victory. Where O death, is your victory? Where, O death, is your sting?' And so the future Paul looks forward to is when 'the last trumpet will sound, and the dead will be raised imperishable, and we will be changed' (1 Cor. 15.52). We will begin our discussion with Paul's use of Habakkuk 2.4 and his understanding of faith.

Faith

We have already seen how Paul links Habakkuk 2.4 (lit. 'The righteous by faith will live') with Genesis 15.6 ('Abraham believed God, and it was reckoned to him as righteousness') in both Romans and Galatians. These are the only two verses in the Old Testament that specifically link faith (*pistis*) or believing (*pisteuo*) with righteousness (*dikaiosyne*). In Galatians, Paul begins with the Abraham text (Gal. 3.6) and links it with Habakkuk 2.4 (Gal. 3.11) rather than texts from the law. In Romans, Paul begins with Habakkuk 2.4 (Rom. 1.17), demonstrates that no one gains righteousness by the law (Rom. 1.18—3.31), and then offers an exposition of Abraham's faith in Romans 4. In both cases Paul's exposition of faith is primarily focused on the Abraham story, so it is reasonable to ask what the Habakkuk text adds to Paul's exposition.

The most obvious answer is that it portrays a different aspect of faith. Abraham is asked to leave his homeland and believe that God is not only able to give him a new land but also a multitude of descendants. Habakkuk is in a rather different situation. Israel has now become numerous and has lived for many centuries in covenant with God, but now faces annihilation by the Chaldeans. The prophet cries out, 'Destruction and violence are before me, strife and contention arise' (Hab. 1.3). In particular, the prophet cannot comprehend why God is 'silent when the wicked swallow those more righteous than they' (Hab. 1.13), and so stations himself on the rampart and demands an answer from God. This is the reply:

Then the LORD answered me and said: Write the vision; make it plain on tablets, so that a runner may read it. For there is still a vision for the appointed time; it speaks of the end, and does not lie. If it seems to tarry, wait for it; it will surely come, it will not delay. Look at the proud! Their spirit is not right in them, *but the righteous live by their faith*. Moreover, wealth is treacherous; the arrogant do not endure. They open their throats wide as Sheol; like Death they never have enough. They gather all nations for themselves, and collect all peoples as their own.

(Hab. 2.2–5)

Now as we have seen, the question of God's faithfulness to Israel is a major theme in Romans. Could it be that Paul's quotation of Habakkuk 2.4 is not simply a summary of the gospel ('righteousness'/ 'justification by faith') but is intended to evoke the theodicy theme of Habakkuk? Hays thinks so, noting that for both Paul and Habakkuk, doubts have been raised about God's faithfulness to Israel because of the apparent success of Gentiles. Of course, there is a big difference between the military threat of the Chaldeans and the success of the Gentile mission, but if the background of Romans is that Gentile Christians are despising Jews (see Romans 11.17–24), this might be more understandable. On the other hand, Paul does not quote any other text from Habakkuk, and one can reasonably ask whether his readers in Rome could have deduced all this from a single six-word quotation, especially as Habakkuk is not mentioned by name. It may be that Paul is simply struck by the almost formulaic summary that 'The righteous by faith will live' (see Appendix 3 for the Qumran commentary on these verses).

Boasting in the Lord

Paul's argument in 1 Corinthians 1—3 is that God's plan to redeem humankind turns the world's values upside down. It is not how the wise or clever would have done it, and indeed this is the very reason they reject it (1 Cor. 2.8). Paul finds confirmation of this in a number of texts that state that God has thwarted the wisdom of the wise (Isa. 29.14), that a great gulf exists between his wisdom and all human wisdom (Isa. 40.13) and that he reveals his plans to those who were least expecting it (Isa. 64.4). All this should result in an attitude expressed in Jeremiah 9.23–24: 'Do not let the wise boast in their wisdom, do not let the mighty boast in their might, do not let the wealthy boast in their wealth; but let those who boast boast in this, that they understand and know me, that I am the LORD.' Paul quotes this in 1 Corinthians 1.31 by means of a short summary: 'Let the one who boasts, boast in the Lord.'[1] This could mean that they are to 'boast in what the Lord does' or 'boast in who the Lord is', but what follows suggests that the emphasis is christological. One of Paul's frequent expressions is that Christians are 'in Christ', that is, their life now derives from Christ. Paul can even say in Galatians 2.20 that he no longer lives but Christ lives in him. Thus to 'boast in the Lord' is not just to boast about the Lord but to affirm that one's whole being is rooted 'in the Lord', that is, 'in Christ'. So having reminded them of their own humble origins ('not many of you were wise by human standards, not many were powerful, not many were of noble birth'), he affirms that God has nevertheless chosen them (1 Cor. 1.28) and become the source of their life in Christ (1 Cor. 1.30). They should not therefore be swayed by the arguments of the eloquent and clever but remain rooted in Christ, who is the wisdom of God.

Paul quotes Jeremiah 9.23–24 again in 2 Corinthians 10.17, but with a somewhat different emphasis. It would appear that some in Corinth are challenging Paul's authority and would rather follow more 'gifted' apostles. In response, Paul allows himself a boast, though he knows such talk is foolish (2 Cor. 11.16). Whatever credentials they possess, Paul can match them. But if he must boast, he will boast in his hardships because that is when the power of God is most clearly visible. In this way, though he would rather not have been goaded into such boasting, he still abides by the principle of Jeremiah 9.23–24, which he explains thus: 'For it is not those who commend themselves that are approved, but those whom the Lord commends' (2 Cor. 10.18). God has in fact done significant things through Paul and it is legitimate to point this out (when his authority is opposed), provided that the emphasis is on what God has done. As Jeremiah 9.23–24 makes clear, there is no place for boasting in one's own accomplishments; one should only boast in the knowledge of God and what he has done and what he continues to do.

Spiritual discernment

If God's truth is not discovered by human wisdom and cleverness, how is it discerned? In 1 Corinthians 2, Paul asserts that it can only be known if the Spirit makes it known. Just as the human spirit knows about human things, so God's Spirit knows about the 'depths of God' (1 Cor. 2.10). But this is not just a question of an external agency imparting knowledge, for Christians have received the Spirit of God. They have thus become spiritual beings (*pneumatikoi*) and hence can discern spiritual things (*pneumatika*). This is why Paul can apply Isaiah 64.4 to the Christians at Corinth: 'From ages past no one has heard, no ear has perceived, no eye has seen any God besides you, who works for those who wait for him.' Paul's quotation in 1 Corinthians 2.9 only picks up the key words of this passage, and says that truth is imparted to 'those who love him' rather than to 'those who wait for him' (or the LXX's 'those who wait for mercy' – see Appendix 1). For this reason some scholars think Paul has a number of texts in mind, including the apocryphal book of Sirach, which is part of the LXX. Many of its themes resonate with the opening chapters of 1 Corinthians:

> All wisdom is from the Lord, and with him it remains for ever... The height of heaven, the breadth of the earth, the abyss, and wisdom – who can search them out?... There is but one who is wise, greatly to be feared, seated upon his throne – the Lord. It is he who created her; he saw her and took her measure; he poured her out upon all his works, upon all the living according to his gift; he lavished her upon those who love him.
>
> (Sir. 1.1–10)

However, Paul wishes to make a more specific claim. He quotes Isaiah 40.13 in the form, 'For who has known the mind of the Lord so as to instruct him?' and then adds: 'But we have the mind of Christ' (1 Cor. 2.16). Isaiah's question is rhetorical and expects the answer: 'No one has known the mind of the Lord'. Indeed, it adds to the case already presented that the wisdom of the wise can never penetrate the mysteries of God, for God thwarts such attempts, as Isaiah 29.14 makes clear: 'The wisdom of their wise shall perish, and the discernment of the discerning shall be hidden.'[2] But God's wisdom is embodied in Christ crucified, and Christians who are united to Christ have the mind of Christ. So in opposition to Isaiah's rhetorical statement that no one can know the mind of the Lord, Paul asserts that it *is* possible for Christians to know it because they have the mind of Christ. This of course picks up the word 'mind' from the quotation, but also looks back to the exhortation in 1 Corinthians 1.10 that they should avoid divisions by having the 'same mind' among them. Paul now clarifies how that is possible: it is the mind of Christ that they should have among them.

The use of tongues and prophecy in worship

In 1 Corinthians 14, Paul addresses a specific problem that has arisen in the Church, namely the role or purpose of speaking in tongues in the worship service. Evidently some were going against Paul's principle of love (1 Cor. 13) by using their gifts to exalt themselves rather than to build up (edify) the congregation. It is easy to see how this might have come about. Speaking in an alien language could easily suggest that such a person has a deeper or more spiritual relationship with God than 'ordinary' Christians, and it is possible that this is one of the causes of division. Paul is not against speaking in tongues (1 Cor. 14.2), and acknowledges that it has value in communicating with God. But unless it is accompanied by interpretation it is gibberish to everyone else. On the other hand, prophecy stands in the great Israelite tradition of making God's will known to the people. This is always of value (1 Cor. 14.3), and benefits the whole congregation. Paul supports this with a quotation from Isaiah 28.11–12 to the effect that even if God were to speak to his people through 'strange tongues' and the 'lips of foreigners', they would still not listen. As with the Habakkuk quotation, there is a considerable difference between the political context of the quotation and the specific divisions in the Church. Perhaps Paul thought he was exercising his own prophetic gift as he changed some of the wording of his quotations and/or combined them with other texts.[3]

Purity and separation

Between 2 Corinthians 6.13 ('open wide your hearts also') and 7.2 ('Make room in your hearts for us; we have wronged no one') there is a paragraph that appears to interrupt the flow of the argument and many scholars believe it did not originally belong there. It concerns purity and separation and is heavily dependent on scriptural quotations and allusions. The paragraph begins with a command not to be mismatched with unbelievers, which is supported by a list of five incongruous partnerships: righteousness/lawlessness; light/darkness; Christ/Beliar;[4] believer/unbeliever; temple of God/idols. It then asserts that 'we are the temple of the living God' and supports it ('as God said') with scriptural quotations drawn from Leviticus 26.12, Ezekiel 37.27, Isaiah 52.11, Ezekiel 20.34 and 2 Samuel 7.14 – see Table 6.1 (where exact agreement in the Greek is indicated by italics, though this agreement is not always apparent in the English).

Table 6.1

2 Corinthians 6.16–18	Old Testament
I will live in them and walk among them, and I will be their God, and they shall be my people.	And I will *walk among* you, *and will be* your *God, and* you *shall be my people.* (Lev. 26.12)
	My dwelling place shall be with them; *and I will be their God, and they shall be my people.* (Ezek. 37.27)
Therefore come out from them, and be separate from them, says the Lord, and touch nothing unclean;	Depart, depart, *go out* from there! *Touch no unclean thing*; *go out* from the midst of it, purify yourselves. (Isa. 52.11)
then I will welcome you,	I will bring you out from the peoples and *gather you* out of the countries where you are scattered. (Ezek. 20.34)
and I will be your father, and you shall be my sons and daughters, says the Lord Almighty.	*I will be* a *father* to him, *and* he *shall be* a *son* to me. (2 Sam. 7.14)

None of these verses specifically mentions the temple, but they are all to do with God making his dwelling place – a word linked with tent or tabernacle – with his people. The purity associated with God's temple is transferred to the Corinthian Christians and thus supports the exhortation in 2 Corinthians 7.1 to be separate: 'Since we have these promises, beloved, let us cleanse ourselves from every defilement of body and spirit, making holiness perfect in the fear of God.'

Paul makes use of this imagery in 1 Corinthians 5—6, though it is not supported by quotations from the prophets. In 1 Corinthians 5, Paul is urging the Corinthians to shun a person who is guilty of an immoral act 'not found even among the pagans' (1 Cor. 5.1). Instead of temple imagery, he uses Passover imagery ('let us celebrate the festival...with the unleavened bread of sincerity and truth'), ending with the expulsion formula (lit. 'drive the evil from among you'), which is frequent in Deuteronomy (see, for example, 17.7; 19.19; 21.21; 22.21). However, in 1 Corinthians 6.19 Paul does use temple imagery: 'do you not know that your body is a temple of the Holy Spirit within you...?' His point is that because Christians are united with Christ, having sex with a prostitute would be like forcing Christ to have sex with a prostitute. In both passages Paul uses Israel's worship traditions to exhort Christians to purity and separation.

Resurrection

Paul begins 1 Corinthians 15 with a list of witnesses to Christ's resurrection, ending with a reference to himself: 'Last of all, as to one untimely born, he appeared also to me.' Evidently some were denying that there would be a future resurrection (1 Cor. 15.12), possibly because they thought the idea sounded primitive. Surely the afterlife would be some sort of merging of our spirits with God (pure energy, as we might say), not a matter of resurrected bodies? Paul's argument for a 'spiritual body' is complex and has already been discussed in Chapter 1 in relation to Adam. What he now adds is the scriptural support for Christ's victory over death. The first passage is Isaiah 25.8, and comes in a section of Isaiah that Paul would have found extremely suggestive:

> And he will destroy on this mountain the shroud that is cast over all peoples, the sheet that is spread over all nations; *he will swallow up death for ever.* Then the Lord GOD will wipe away the tears from all faces, and the disgrace of his people he will take away from all the earth, for the LORD has spoken. It will be said on that day, Lo, this is our God; we have waited for him, so that he might save us. This is the LORD for whom we have waited; let us be glad and rejoice in his salvation.
>
> (Isa. 25.7–9)

Paul only quotes the snippet, 'he will swallow up death for ever', which he renders as a passive and speaks of 'in victory' rather than 'for ever': 'Death has been swallowed up in victory.' These might be deliberate changes by Paul, especially as he appears to have done the same with the following snippet from Hosea 13.14. On the other hand, there are variations in the manuscript tradition for this verse, and we know of at least one Greek text that agrees with Paul, though in its present form it is later than Paul. Either way, the import of the verse supports Paul's claim that the prophets looked forward to a day when death would be no more (the verse is also quoted by the rabbis). Paul's claim is that this has now been realized in Christ's resurrection, which has opened up the path for others to follow, so that when the trumpet sounds, 'this perishable body puts on imperishability, and this mortal body puts on immortality' (1 Cor. 15.54).

The snippet from Hosea 13.14 is more complicated because in the original it appears to be talking about death's victory over sinful Israel. Because of their rebellion, God asks the question, 'Shall I ransom them from the power of Sheol? Shall I redeem them from Death?' (Hos. 13.14). The answer appears to be no, for 'compassion is hidden from my eyes'. Thus the snippet from which Paul quotes – 'O Death, where are your plagues? O Sheol, where is your destruction?' – is a summons for them to come and do their worst, not a statement about their powerlessness. They only become that when Paul combines them with his quotation of Isaiah 25.8:

> When this perishable body puts on imperishability, and this mortal body puts on immortality, then the saying that is written will be fulfilled: *'Death has been swallowed up in victory.' 'Where, O death, is your victory? Where, O death, is your sting?'* The sting of death is sin, and the power of sin is the law. But thanks be to God, who gives us the victory through our Lord Jesus Christ.
>
> (1 Cor. 15.54–57)[5]

Confession and worship of God/Christ

Paul's use of Isaiah 45.23 is enlightening since he applies it to God in Romans 14.11 and to Christ in Philippians 2.11. In Isaiah 45.22, God issues an invitation: 'Turn to me and be saved, all the ends of the earth! For I am God, and there is no other.' This is followed by a statement of the trustworthiness of the saying: 'By myself I have sworn, from my mouth has gone forth in righteousness a word that shall not return.' Then comes the snippet Paul quotes: 'To me every knee shall bow, every tongue shall swear [Gk: confess].' In Romans 14, Paul is discussing matters of conscience (what one shall eat, what days to keep holy), and urges tolerance to those who see things differently. His support for this is, first, that they are people for whom Christ died and therefore of great value; they ought thus to think very carefully before they cause such a person to stumble. Second, he states that we are all accountable before God, which he supports by quoting Isaiah 45.23: 'For we will all stand before the judgement seat of God. For it is written, "As I live, says the Lord, every knee shall bow to me, and every tongue shall give praise [confess] to God"' (Rom. 14.10–11).

The context is similar in Philippians, in that some are thinking too highly of themselves and need a dose of humility. Paul offers the Christ-hymn in Philippians 2.6–11 ('Let the same mind be in you that was [or "is"] in Christ Jesus'), which ends with the statement that 'at the name of Jesus *every knee should bend*, in heaven and on earth and under the earth, and *every tongue should confess* that Jesus Christ is Lord, to the glory of God the Father' (Phil. 2.10–11). There are three differences from Romans 14.11. First, it is 'at the name of Jesus' that every knee will bow/bend. Second, he expands the 'every knee' by adding 'in heaven and on earth and under the earth'. Third, whereas Isaiah 45.23 and Romans 14.11 speak of 'confessing to God', Philippians gives the content of what is to be confessed, namely that 'Jesus Christ is Lord, to the glory of God the Father'. This is interesting in that the ultimate goal remains 'the glory of God', as it is in Isaiah, but what brings glory to God is now stated as confessing that 'Jesus Christ is Lord'.

Paul's own vocation

In isolation, Paul's quotation of Isaiah 49.8 – 'In a time of favour I have answered you, on a day of salvation I have helped you' – looks like a promise that God will hear the prayers of the Corinthians and act upon them (2 Cor. 6.2). However, the original text is referring to the 'servant of God', whose mission is not only to restore Israel but also the nations (Isa. 49.6). Many scholars think that Paul is applying this text to himself and urging the Corinthians not to reject his ministry, for he continues: 'We are putting no obstacle in anyone's way, so that no fault may be found with our ministry, but as servants of God we have commended ourselves in every way' (2 Cor. 6.3). This interpretation would be confirmed if the NRSV is correct in its translation of 2 Corinthians 6.1: 'As we work together with him, we urge you also not to accept the grace of God in vain.' In other words, Paul is in partnership with God, urging the Corinthians not to reject the ministry of reconciliation with which he is charged to preach.

However, as the NRSV footnote on this verse makes clear, the Greek only says, 'As we work together', which could refer to Paul and God or Paul and the Corinthians. What settles it for many scholars is that the description of the servant's birth ('The LORD called me before I was born' – Isa. 49.1) resonates with Paul's description in Galatians 1.15 ('But when God, who had set me apart before I was born') and the servant's frustration ('I have laboured in vain' – Isa. 49.4), while remaining faithful ('yet surely my cause is with the Lord') could be a summary of 2 Corinthians. We could also add Romans 15.21, where Paul quotes Isaiah 52.15 – 'Those who have never been told of him shall see, and those who have never heard of him shall understand' – as his mission statement for pressing on to places where Christ has not been named. It is interesting to speculate as to whether this is the reason Paul – unlike Acts and 1 Peter – does not explicitly quote Isaiah 53 in relation to Christ's vicarious death. Much of the servant role is fulfilled in Paul, although of course he would be the first to point out that it is Christ working through him.

Conclusion

Not only does Paul see the prophets as predicting such things as the inclusion of the Gentiles, Israel's unbelief and future salvation, he also believes that they speak to particular issues in the life of the Church. This includes general issues, such as purity and separation, spiritual discernment and appropriate boasting, as well as specific issues, such as speaking in tongues during the worship service. It would appear that Paul sees his own vocation as similar to the prophets of old, and perhaps also the servant of God in Isaiah 49. Although the use of Isaiah 45.23 in Philippians 2.11 can rightly be called christological interpretation, the majority of quotations are applied to the people of God rather than Christ. Hays called this *ecclesiological* interpretation, though some critics have suggested that Paul would surely have thought of God rather than the Church as the centre of his hermeneutics. Hays responded by coining the term *teleological* interpretation, from the Greek word *telos*, which means 'goal' or 'end'. Paul's interpretation is driven by the belief that God's plan to redeem humanity is being realized in the Church, a community of both Jews and Gentiles. It is his belief that God's *telos* is being realized here and now that characterizes his scriptural interpretations.[6]

7

Paul and the writings

Introduction

As was noted in the introduction to this book, it is possible that the reference to Jesus fulfilling the law, the prophets and the psalms in Luke 24.44 refers to the three-fold division of the – later – Hebrew Bible, with psalms named as the most prominent member of the writings. On the other hand, Luke 24.25 rebukes the disciples for being slow to believe 'all that the prophets have declared', and verse 27 says that 'beginning with Moses and all the prophets, he interpreted to them the things about himself in all the scriptures'.[1] Our chapter title, then, is more a matter of convenience than the suggestion that Paul thought the psalms were a different type of literature from the prophets. As we shall see below, Paul's quotations of the psalms can largely be explained by the same categories that we have used for the prophets: proclamation of the gospel; inclusion of the Gentiles; current unbelief of the Jews; future salvation; Paul's vocation and particular issues facing the Church. They are seldom quoted as expressions of praise (Rom. 15.9, 11) and are certainly not confined to 'liturgical' contexts.

There are around 19 explicit quotations of the psalms in Paul's undisputed letters, along with two references to Job (5.13; 35.7), one to Proverbs (25.21–22) and possibly one to Ecclesiastes (7.20). The 19 quotations of the psalms are found in Romans (14), 1 Corinthians (3) and 2 Corinthians (2), and are drawn from the following psalms: 5, 8, 10, 14, 18, 19, 24, 32, 36, 44, 51, 69, 94, 112, 116, 117, 140. Two things are interesting about this list. First, only Psalm 8 and Psalm 69 are quoted elsewhere in the New Testament, so the majority appear to come from Paul's own exegetical work. Second, the psalms that are quoted most frequently in the New Testament (2, 110, 118) are not quoted by Paul, again suggesting an independent mind at work. Having said that, he shares with Jewish tradition the belief that David is the author of the psalms, and although he does not name him as frequently as Isaiah (which he names five times), he is explicitly said to speak (Rom. 4.6) and say (Rom. 11.9) through the quoted psalm texts.

Paul's use of the psalms

Proclamation of the gospel

In Romans 10, Paul argues that the gospel he preaches is 'near you, on your lips and in your heart' (a text originally referring to the law), and that this gospel has gone out to all the world. He cites Isaiah 52.7 to emphasize the wonder of this ('How beautiful are the feet of those who bring good news') and Isaiah 53.1 to show that Scripture recognizes that not all will believe it ('Lord, who has believed our message?'). Paul anticipates a possible response to this – 'they do not believe because they have not heard' – and refutes it by citing Psalm 19.4: 'Their voice has gone out to all the earth, and their words to the ends of the world.' The psalm is a eulogy to the heavens, 'telling of the glory of God' (Ps. 19.1), but Paul applies the plurals ('their voice', 'their words') to himself and his fellow preachers. Many scholars think Paul has simply borrowed the words for rhetorical effect, but Wagner holds that it is more sophisticated than that. The psalm continues with a eulogy to the law, and Paul's earlier citations show that he thought the law was a witness to the gospel. Thus Wagner suggests that '"their voice...their words" refer at once to the message "spoken" by creation, the message of the Law, and the message of Paul and his associates'.[2] Whether or not this is true, Paul thinks that Psalm 19.4 is scriptural proof that the good news has been universally proclaimed and unbelief is therefore culpable.

Inclusion of the Gentiles

Many scholars regard Romans 15.7–13 as the climax of the letter, combining the themes of God's faithfulness to Israel and the inclusion of the Gentiles. In terms reminiscent of what Paul says about Abraham's dual role (Rom. 4.11–12), he says that Christ (or 'the Christ') has become a servant of the circumcised, 'in order that he might confirm the promises given to the patriarchs' (Rom. 15.8), and a servant of the Gentiles in order that they 'might glorify God for his mercy' (Rom. 15.9). He supports these statements by a string of quotations drawn from Psalm 18.49, Deuteronomy 32.43, Psalm 117.1 and Isaiah 11.10, all of which speak of Gentiles (*ethne*). Of the two psalm quotations, Psalm 117.1 is the most straightforward. It belongs to a short collection of psalms (113—118) known as the *Hallel* ('Praise'), which according to the Mishnah, were sung at the major festivals. Psalm 117 only consists of two verses and encapsulates the themes of God's faithfulness and the inclusion of the Gentiles: 'Praise the LORD, all you nations! Extol him, all you peoples! For great is his steadfast love toward us, and the faithfulness of the LORD endures for ever. Praise the LORD!' Hebrew parallelism suggests that 'nations' and 'peoples' refer to the same group, but it is possible that Paul saw here a veiled prophecy (like the singular 'seed' discussed in Galatians 3.16 – see p. 41) that spoke of Gentiles (nations) and Jews (peoples). Even if this is not the case, Paul knows a psalm that invites the Gentiles to join with Israel in praising God, and he thinks that it is the Christ-event that has made this possible.

The other psalm quotation comes from the penultimate verse of Psalm 18: 'For this I will extol you, O LORD, among the nations, and sing praises to your name.' The ascription at the beginning of the psalm calls it a 'psalm of David', but who does Paul think the 'I' refers to when he quotes it in Romans 15.9? It could be himself, but given what he has just said about Christ becoming a servant to Jews and Gentiles, it is likely that he understands it to be Christ. Two things support this. First, earlier in the chapter (verse 3) Paul states that 'Christ did not please himself', and supports it by a quotation from Psalm 69.9: 'the insults of those who insult you have fallen on me'. There can be no doubt that Paul understands Christ as the 'me' of the quotation, and it is therefore an explicitly christological interpretation. Second, the final verse of Psalm 18 says: 'Great triumphs he gives to his king, and shows steadfast love to his anointed [*christos*], to David and his descendants [*sperma*] for ever.' This would have strongly suggested to Paul, reading the psalm in Greek, that it refers to Christ, the seed of David (Rom. 1.3).

This is not Paul's only christological interpretation of Scripture. We have seen how he identifies the 'seed' of Abraham as a reference to Christ (Gal. 3.16), along with the rock that supplied water to the wilderness generation (1 Cor. 10.4). However, seeing Christ in the psalms adds another dimension, for Paul appears to think that the words attributed to David – as implied by the ascription of the psalm – were actually spoken by Christ. This is different from the claim that because David was a prophet, he was enabled to speak about the resurrection of the messiah (Acts 2.31, citing Ps. 16.10). Here, it is being claimed that David's words – 'the insults of those who insult you have fallen on me' – are actually the words of Christ. Anthony Hanson takes this literally, and thinks that Paul envisages this as a pre-incarnate dialogue between God the Father and God the Son.[3] Others have preferred a less metaphysical interpretation, suggesting that Paul understood the psalms to contain the 'prayers of the messiah' (when he comes).[4] The close connection between David as God's anointed (*christos*) and Jesus Christ, who is of the 'seed' of David (Rom. 1.3), facilitates such an interpretative move. It is thus the messiah who will cry out, 'for my thirst they gave me vinegar to drink' (Ps. 69.21), 'into your hand I commit my spirit' (Ps. 31.5) and 'My God, my God, why have you forsaken me?' (Ps. 22.1). Of course, not everything in the psalms can be seen as the 'prayers of the messiah', for sometimes David is confessing his sin (Ps. 51). So if David is an inspired prophet, Paul is an inspired listener, who discerns the 'prayers of the messiah' *among* the words of David.

Also important for Paul's theme of the inclusion of the Gentiles is his allusion to Psalm 143.2b in Romans 3.20. The words are not introduced as a quotation, but most scholars are persuaded that there is enough similarity with the LXX to make the allusion certain. Paul has just listed a string of quotations to the effect that all are sinful (Rom. 3.10–18). He then makes a deduction that he supports by an allusion to Psalm 143.2 (see Table 7.1).

Table 7.1

Psalm 143.2 LXX	Romans 3.19–20
lit. And do not enter into judgement with your servant	lit. We know that whatever the law says, it says to those who are under the law, so that every mouth may be silenced, and the whole world held accountable to God.
because	Because *by works of law*
no living being	no flesh
will be justified	will be justified
before you.	before him.

Readers unfamiliar with the psalm might assume that the quoted text speaks of 'works of law', but this is Paul's interpretative comment. What the psalm does say is that no living being will be justified before God, and thus Paul's addition is intended as a clarification. If no living being will be justified before God then that includes those who claim to be in a covenantal relationship with God and demonstrate it by 'works of law'.

Current unbelief of the Jews

As Paul outlines the reasons for Israel's current state of unbelief, he takes up the idea of divine hardening in Romans 11.7: 'The elect obtained it, but the rest were hardened.' He quotes first from Isaiah 29.10 – 'God gave them a sluggish spirit, eyes that would not see and ears that would not hear, down to this very day' – and then Psalm 69.22–23: 'Let their table become a snare and a trap...Let their eyes be darkened so that they cannot see, and make their loins tremble continually.' It is likely that the two verses are connected in Paul's mind by the reference to eyes that cannot see, though it is clear from the rest of the New Testament that Psalm 69 was understood to be speaking about Christ and his enemies.[5]

We have already mentioned the collection of proof texts in Romans 3.10–18, but now we shall look at them in more detail. Psalm 14.1–3 encapsulates much of what Paul wants to say about the human condition (the words he quotes are in italics):

> Fools say in their hearts, 'There is no God.'
> They are corrupt, they do abominable deeds; *there is no one who does good.*
> The LORD looks down from heaven on humankind
> to see if there are *any who are wise, who seek after God.*
> *They have all gone astray, they are all alike perverse;*
> *there is no one who does good, no, not one.*
>
> (Ps. 14.1–3)

The last line prompts Paul to remove the quest ('to see if there are any') and make the whole thing an indictment ('There is no one who is righteous, not even one'), perhaps drawing on Ecclesiastes 7.20: 'Surely there is no one on earth so righteous as to do good without ever sinning.' He then follows this with snippets from a number of psalms (5.9; 140.3; 10.7; 36.1) concerning the wicked, especially evil speech: 'Their *throats* are opened graves; they use their *tongues* to deceive. The venom of vipers is under their *lips*. Their *mouths* are full of cursing and bitterness.' The progression from throats, tongues, lips, mouth suggests that some care has gone into its construction, and some scholars believe that Paul is quoting an existing collection rather than spontaneously generating it as he dictates the letter (Rom. 16.22). One of the reasons for this is that if we look at the psalms that are quoted, the negative statements are all aimed at the wicked (just as Psalm 14 is aimed at 'fools'), whereas the author of the psalm believes that he belongs to the company of the righteous.[6] How then can Paul think that they support his universal indictment?

James Dunn has argued that central to Paul's understanding is the fact that the gospel has removed the distinction between Jew and Gentile. That is why he can take texts that were originally aimed at Jews and apply them to Gentiles (Hos. 1.10; 2.23, in Rom. 9.25–26), and texts that were originally applied to Gentiles ('the wicked') and apply them to Jews.[7] This is a neat solution, but there is probably more to it than this. Paul wishes to show 'that all, both Jews and Greeks, are under the power of sin' (Rom. 3.9), but he does not want to suggest that God no longer distinguishes between good and evil. It is more that 'good' – or righteousness – has been redefined in the light of the Christ-event. So Paul's use of these psalms may have a double aspect: when brought under the umbrella of Psalm 14.1–3 (or Eccles. 7.20) they speak of universal sin; but when read on their own terms they speak of God as a refuge for the righteous and an enemy of the wicked. Both themes are necessary for Paul's understanding of salvation in Christ.[8]

Future salvation

Paul's climactic saying that in the end, 'all Israel will be saved' (Rom. 11.26), is supported by two quotations from Isaiah (59.20–21; 27.7). Before that, Paul has used Psalm 51.4 and Psalm 94.14 to support the view that God is faithful and will never abandon Israel. In Romans 3, Paul argues that even though some of Israel have proved unfaithful, this does not change the faithfulness of God. In somewhat exaggerated terms (known as hyperbole), he says: 'Although everyone is a liar, let God be proved true, as it is written, "So that you may be justified in your words, and prevail in your judging."' The quotation is taken from Psalm 51.4 which, according to the ascription, concerns

David's penitence for his sin with Bathsheba. David acknowledges that his sin is against God, and that if it were a court case, God would be justified in passing sentence. The quoted words assert that God's words and judgements will be proved right (the meaning of justified here), but Paul may also be influenced by the context: if this is true when David sinned, it is certainly true if some of Israel have proved unfaithful.

Paul returns to the theme of God's faithfulness and Israel's salvation in Romans 9—11. After outlining Israel's failure in Romans 9—10, he opens Romans 11 with a rhetorical question: 'I ask then, has God rejected his people?' He immediately rejects such an idea ('By no means!'), and offers three reasons in support. The first is that Paul himself is an Israelite, though one person might not seem like much of a fulfilment. The third – we will look at the second in a moment – cites the example of Elijah, who complained that he was the only faithful Israelite left, but God told him that there were 7,000 others who had remained faithful. Paul doesn't make the connection explicit, but perhaps he is applying the Elijah example to himself. At times, he has felt like the only one left, but (no doubt) God has 7,000 more like him.

In between these two examples Paul asserts that: 'God has not rejected his people whom he foreknew.' Now this could be Paul's own statement, but most scholars think he is drawing on Psalm 94.14: 'For the LORD will not forsake his people; he will not abandon his heritage.' If so, then Paul has interpreted 'heritage' as those whom God 'foreknew', a rare word that was introduced into the discussion in Romans 8.29: 'For those whom he foreknew he also predestined to be conformed to the image of his Son, in order that he might be the firstborn within a large family.' The psalm asserts that despite persecution by evildoers, God will not forsake his people. It is not directly addressing the question of what God will do if Israel proves unfaithful, but Paul deduces from words like 'heritage' that Israel will never be abandoned.

We saw in the previous chapter how Paul uses quotations from Isaiah and Hosea to show that Christ has defeated death. Prior to that, Paul draws on Psalm 8.6 – 'God has put all things in subjection under his feet' (1 Cor. 15.27) – to show that all enemies, including death, will be subjugated. The psalm is referring to the wonders of creation – 'When I look at your heavens, the work of your fingers' –

and human beings, who were made 'a little lower than God' but crowned with 'glory and honour' (Ps. 8.5). Verse 6 – 'You have given them dominion over the works of your hands; you have put all things under their feet' – is thus a reference to the dominion granted to humankind in Genesis 1.26. How then does Paul apply this to the eschatological victory where all things will be subjected to Christ? This is best seen by quoting the RSV instead of the inclusive (plural) language of the NRSV, along with the use made of this text in Hebrews, once thought to be by Paul (KJV) but accepted as anonymous today (see Table 7.2 – parallels indicated by italics).

What is interesting about this comparison is that both Paul and Hebrews apply the text to Christ and follow it with an explanation about the meaning of 'all things in subjection'. Paul makes the point that the 'all things' of the quotation clearly does not refer to God, the one who is subjecting all things, and concludes that in the end, even Christ will be subject to God. This somewhat stark subordinationism, which was naturally a point of debate in later disputes about the divinity of Christ, is possibly mitigated by the final statement that 'God may be everything to everyone', if Paul understands Christ to be included in the reference to God.[9]

Hebrews is also concerned about the scope of the 'all things', but is more interested in the point that we do not see this subjection at present. However, Hebrews is far more ambiguous as to whether the psalm applies directly to Christ or refers to humanity's subjection of all things. This is most evident in the phrase, 'But we see Jesus', which is rather odd if the previous phrase – 'we do not yet see everything in subjection to him' – is also a reference to Jesus. It would appear that the ambiguity as to whether words for 'man' are singular ('Adam', 'the man') or corporate (humankind) has facilitated the application to Christ.[10]

Paul's vocation and issues in the Church

Romans 8 continues the theme of God's faithfulness but gives it a specifically christological focus: 'If God is for us, who is against us? He who did not withhold his own Son, but gave him up for all of us, will he not with him also give us everything else?' (Rom. 8.31–32). However, Paul's vocation has involved suffering and persecution, and he sees this as a fulfilment of Psalm 44.22: 'For your sake we are being killed all day long; we are accounted as sheep to be slaughtered.' The words translated as 'For your sake' (*heneken sou*) denote purpose,

Table 7.2

Psalm 8.4–6 RSV	1 Corinthians 15.25–26 RSV	Hebrews 2.6–9 RSV
what is man that thou art mindful of him, and the son of man that thou dost care for him? Yet thou hast made him little less than God [or angels], and dost crown him with glory and honour.		*'What is man that thou art mindful of him, or the son of man, that thou carest for him? Thou didst make him for a little while lower than the angels, thou hast crowned him with glory and honour,*
Thou hast given him dominion over the works of thy hands; thou hast put all things under his feet,	For he must reign until he has put all his enemies under his feet. The last enemy to be destroyed is death. 'For God has put all things in subjection under his feet.'	*putting everything in subjection under his feet.'*
all sheep and oxen, and also the beasts of the field, the birds of the air, and the fish of the sea, whatever passes along the paths of the sea.	But when it says, 'All things are put in subjection under him,' it is plain that he is excepted who put all things under him. When all things are subjected to him, then the Son himself will also be subjected to him who put all things under him, that God may be everything to every one.	Now in putting everything in subjection to him, he left nothing outside his control. As it is, we do not yet see everything in subjection to him. But we see Jesus, who for *a little while was made lower than the angels, crowned with glory and honour* because of the suffering of death, so that by the grace of God he might taste death for every one.

and could equally be translated as 'because of you'. This appears to be the psalmist's meaning, as can be seen from the following verse: 'Rouse yourself! Why do you sleep, O Lord?' The psalmist is citing God as the cause of his suffering, and he wants it to stop: 'Rise up, come to our help.' Paul is not calling for it to stop, rather he gladly accepts such things as part of his vocation, believing that nothing can separate him – and his fellow believers – from the love of God (Rom. 8.37–39). The ambiguity of the Greek phrase *heneken sou* allows Paul to quote the text as predicting his and his fellow Christians' suffering, without blaming God for it.

The imagery of 'sheep to be slaughtered' is also found in the suffering servant text of Isaiah 53.7. Quotations from Isaiah 53 are explicitly applied to Christ in Matthew 8.17, Luke 22.37, Acts 8.32–3 and 1 Peter 2.22–25, and may well lie behind the 'ransomed for many' and 'poured out for many' sayings in Mark's Gospel (Mark 10.45; 14.24). Some have argued that it lies behind such passages as Romans 4.25 ('handed over to death') and Philippians 2.7–8 ('emptied himself … obedient unto death'), but it has always puzzled commentators as to why Paul does not make such connections explicit. One answer to this could be that he saw himself and his fellow preachers as suffering servants ('sheep to be slaughtered'), giving their lives in service to God. Of course, in doing so they are following in the footsteps of Christ, but it may be that this corporate understanding of the servant was more important to Paul than a specifically christological one (see also p. 96).

Similarly, Paul states in 2 Corinthians 4.11 that: 'For while we live, we are always being given up to death for Jesus' sake, so that the life of Jesus may be made visible in our mortal flesh.' He then applies the words of the LXX of Psalm 116.10 – 'I believed, and so I spoke' – to himself and his fellow preachers. It is easy to see why Paul might have been drawn to this psalm:

> The snares of death encompassed me; the pangs of Sheol laid hold on me; I suffered distress and anguish. Then I called on the name of the Lord…Gracious is the Lord…you have delivered my soul from death, my eyes from tears, my feet from stumbling. I walk before the Lord in the land of the living. *I kept my faith, even when I said, 'I am greatly afflicted'*…Precious in the sight of the Lord is the death of his faithful ones. O Lord, I am your servant.
>
> (Ps. 116.3–16)

However, Paul's quotation – 'I believed, and so I spoke' – is from the
LXX, and there are two significant differences from the Hebrew
(and hence the NRSV quoted above). First, the Hebrew text supplies
the content of what is spoken ('I am greatly afflicted'), and
Paul would hardly wish to state that this is what he preaches. The
LXX, on the other hand, does not have this phrase but simply says,
'I believed, and so I spoke', which allows Paul to make the identification, 'we also believe, and so we speak' (2 Cor. 4.13b). Second,
these words in the LXX are not in the middle of Psalm 116, as in
the Hebrew, but actually form the first verse of a new psalm. Thus
although Psalm 116.1–9 appears to be very relevant to Paul's
situation, his quotation is actually from the next psalm (as set out in
the LXX).

This raises an important methodological question as to what the
original recipients would have made of such a quotation. It is unlikely
that they would know the Hebrew text, and so they would have
treated Paul's words as the first line of a psalm that confidently says,
'I believed, and so I spoke', especially as Paul follows it with the words,
'we also believe, and so we speak'. So if we use the first part of Psalm
116 to suggest that Paul was identifying with the distressed yet faithful figure of its author, it is almost certain that his original recipients
would not have perceived this. We can then suggest three possible
scenarios: first, the background was important for Paul but it is not
why he is quoting the text; second, the background was important
for Paul and he hoped that the Corinthians would perceive it; third,
the background was not important for Paul since he has not made
it explicit for the Corinthians. As we shall see in our final chapter,
the view that one takes on this affects the way one approaches the
study of Paul's use of Scripture.

In 2 Corinthians 9, Paul is urging the Corinthians to be generous
in the collection for the poor (first discussed in 1 Cor. 16). He uses
three arguments, followed by a quotation from Psalm 112.9. The first
argument is the principle that 'the one who sows sparingly will also
reap sparingly, and the one who sows bountifully will also reap bountifully' (2 Cor. 9.6). Now this could just be a popular aphorism, but
the second argument – 'God loves a cheerful giver' – suggests that
Paul may have the book of Proverbs in mind. The words are similar
to the LXX of Proverbs 22.8 (lit. 'God blesses a cheerful and generous
man'). They are missing from the Hebrew text, but the previous

phrase (lit. 'he who sows what is bad, will reap what is evil') is close to 2 Corinthians 9.6. Paul may also have Proverbs 11.24 in mind, which says: 'Some give freely, yet grow all the richer; others withhold what is due, and only suffer want.' Many commentators believe that Paul drew from both of these wisdom texts as he formulated his argument for Christian generosity.

The third argument is the promise that 'God is able to provide you with every blessing in abundance', and is supported by a quotation from Psalm 112.9: 'He scatters abroad, he gives to the poor; his righteousness endures for ever.' Although this seems straightforward, there has been considerable debate as to whether Paul is applying this psalm to God or to the believer. In favour of the former, God is the subject of both the preceding verse ('God is able to provide…') and the verse that follows: 'He who supplies seed to the sower and bread for food will supply and multiply your seed.' On the other hand, there is no doubt that the psalm is referring to the righteous person who scatters abroad and gives to the poor, and Paul refers to 'your righteousness' in the next verse. Thus if the Corinthians are familiar with Psalm 112, they will be inclined to take Paul's words as referring to themselves. If they are not familiar with it, they are likely to take it as a reference to God, once again raising the question of how much scriptural knowledge Paul could assume from the Corinthians.

Paul's use of Proverbs

As well as the allusions to Proverbs in 2 Corinthians 9, in Romans 12.20 Paul has an explicit – somewhat abbreviated – quotation of Proverbs 25.21–22: 'If your enemies are hungry, give them bread to eat; and if they are thirsty, give them water to drink; for you will heap coals of fire on their heads.' The main difficulty is deciding what Paul means by the quotation. The first two clauses are acts of kindness, but the consequences ('heap coals of fire on their heads') suggests vengeance, which contradicts what Paul says in the previous verse ('Beloved, never avenge yourselves') and the following verse ('Do not be overcome by evil, but overcome evil with good'). Charles Barrett concludes that: 'it can scarcely be doubted that the "burning coals" are the fire of remorse. If an enemy is treated in this way he may well be overcome in the best possible fashion – he may become a friend.'[11]

On the other hand, Gordon Zerbe points out that references to 'coals' or 'coals of fire' in the Old Testament are always negative, and that Paul's other uses of 'fire' (1 Cor. 3.13, 15; 2 Thess. 1.8) refer to eschatological judgement. The suggested actions are not acts of vengeance but nor are they attempts at reconciliation. As Romans 12.19 states, vengeance belongs to God.[12]

Paul's use of Job

In Paul's discussion of the inability of human wisdom to understand God (1 Cor. 1—3), he quotes Isaiah 29.14 ('I will destroy the wisdom of the wise'), Psalm 94.11 ('The Lord knows the thoughts of the wise, that they are futile') and Job 5.13 ('He catches the wise in their craftiness'). Like Isaiah 29.14, Job 5.12–13 is not simply pointing out the limitations of human wisdom but asserting that God actively opposes it: 'He frustrates the devices of the crafty, so that their hands achieve no success. He takes the wise in their own craftiness; and the schemes of the wily are brought to a quick end.' Paul's quotation differs considerably from the LXX that has come down to us, which could be deliberate or possibly evidence that he was using a different LXX text. As we will see below, the text of his other quotation from Job is not straightforward either.

In the hymn of praise – known as a 'doxology' – that brings the argument of Romans 9—11 to a close, Paul quotes Isaiah 40.13 ('For who has known the mind of the Lord? Or who has been his counsellor?') and Job 35.7 ('Or who has given a gift to him, to receive a gift in return?'). It is interesting that Paul also quotes this Isaiah text in 1 Corinthians 2.16: he clearly sees connections between these 'wisdom' texts in Isaiah, Psalms and Job. However, the Job quotation is problematic for two reasons. First, the Hebrew text – 'what do you give to him; or what does he receive from your hand?' – says nothing about God repaying the gift, but uses parallelism to say the same thing in a different way. Second, this is one of a number of verses of the LXX that Origen (*c.* 200 CE) marked as absent from the LXX text known to him. It is thus doubtful whether Paul knew the words from a Greek text. Combined with the above, it seems very unlikely that Paul's readers could have known an actual text that contained these quotations, and perhaps he is translating the Hebrew for himself.

Origen's Hexapla

Origen was the greatest textual critic of his day. He constructed a Hexapla of six columns containing the Hebrew text, a transliteration in Greek letters, the LXX and three other Greek versions known as Aquila, Symmachus and Theodotion. Following ancient practices, he marked with an asterisk or obelisk – for omissions and additions respectively – those words or phrases that did not correspond with anything in the Hebrew text. Unfortunately, when there were gaps in the LXX he filled them with phrases from the other versions (mainly Theodotion), and this column was often transmitted as 'the LXX' without the textual markers. Thus we have LXX manuscripts that contain readings that were not in the LXX known to Origen. For example, in the surrounding verses to Job 35.7, the following verses are marked with an asterisk in NETS: 34.3–7, 11b, 18b, 23a, 25b, 28–33; 35.7b–10a, 12a, 15–16. It has been calculated that in Job 32—37 the Greek text known to Origen was 35 per cent shorter than the Hebrew text that has come down to us. For more detail, see the introduction to Job in NETS.

Conclusion

Two points stand out from our analysis in this chapter. First, although Paul draws on wisdom themes from Proverbs and Job, he is just as likely to find them in Isaiah and Psalms. Second, although Paul quotes from the psalms as an expression of praise in Romans 15.9, 11, the majority of his uses fall under the same categories as the prophets: proclamation of the gospel; inclusion of the Gentiles; current unbelief of the Jews; future salvation; Paul's vocation and particular issues facing the Church. Of particular interest is his christological use of Psalm 8.6 ('you have put all things under his feet'), Psalm 69.9 ('the insults of those who insult you have fallen on me') and Psalm 18.49 ('For I will extol you, O LORD, among the nations'). Precisely how Paul understood 'Christ in the psalms' remains a matter for debate.

8

Modern approaches to Paul's use of Scripture

Introduction

In our study of Paul's explicit quotations we have taken an eclectic view, using whatever methods or approaches were helpful for understanding the particular quotation. However, in order to understand *what* scholars are saying about Paul's use of Scripture it is necessary to delineate the particular method or approach being used. In this chapter we will look at three such approaches, which we will call intertextual, narrative and rhetorical:

- An intertextual approach focuses on the surrounding context from which the quote is taken. It argues that a text is not a discreet packet of meaning but belongs to a web or matrix of other texts. Thus a quotation brings with it more than just the cited words; it also brings connotations and associations from the surrounding verses (and verses with similar wording).
- A narrative approach adopts a similar principle but suggests that what a text brings with it is not so much the *local* context but the *narrative* framework to which it belongs. For example, the quotation of Genesis 15.6 – 'Abraham believed God and it was reckoned to him as righteousness' – might well evoke Abraham's life story, but not necessarily the particulars of the surrounding verses.
- A rhetorical approach focuses on what Paul does with the text in order to persuade his readers to accept his interpretation. It might be true that a text can bring with it a variety of associations and connotations, but a rhetorical approach focuses on those things to which Paul draws attention (and not those things he conceals).

Intertextual approaches

Richard Hays

One of the most influential books on Paul's use of Scripture is *Echoes of Scripture in the Letters of Paul* by Richard Hays.[1] As the title suggests, Hays argues that Paul's engagement with Scripture goes far deeper than his explicit quotations. These are just the tip of the iceberg, a marker to indicate which section of the scriptural landscape he is currently roaming. For example, we have seen how Paul refers to Habakkuk 2.4 (lit. 'The righteous by faith will live') in his announcement of the gospel in Romans 1.17. But before Paul cites Habakkuk 2.4 he says: 'For I am not ashamed of the gospel; it is the power of God for salvation to everyone who has faith, to the Jew first and also to the Greek. For in it the righteousness of God is revealed through faith for faith.' Hays suggests that Paul has not formulated this statement in a vacuum but has the LXX of Psalm 98.2–3 in mind:

> The LORD has made known his *salvation*;
> In the presence of the *nations* he has *revealed* his *righteousness*.
> He has remembered his mercy to Jacob
> And his truthfulness to the house of *Israel*.
> All the ends of the earth have seen the *salvation* of our *God*.[2]

Not only does this psalm echo the key terms in Romans 1.16 (*salvation, righteousness, God's revelation, the nations*), its message is that God has made this known to both Jews ('mercy to Jacob') and Gentiles ('ends of the earth'). Indeed, it anticipates Paul's major discussion of God's faithfulness to Israel in Romans 9—11, which culminates in Romans 11.32: 'For God has imprisoned all in disobedience so that he may be *merciful* to all.' But what is different in Hays's analysis is that he does not present this as yet another proof text for Paul's gospel; rather he turns to literature and poetry to describe the subtle effects of such echoes. The psalm verses sound a 'tone whose echo rebounds with greater force than the original sound...his evocation of the psalmist's language hints at a conviction that he articulates explicitly elsewhere: God's grace in Jesus Christ simultaneously extends salvation to the Gentiles and confirms Israel's trust in God's saving righteousness'.[3]

He further notes that many commentators have taken Paul's opening words – 'For I am not ashamed of the gospel' – as the natural embarrassment one might feel about believing in a crucified messiah, but this ignores the important role that 'shame' plays in Scripture. Indeed, Paul will later quote from Isaiah 28.16 that the one who trusts in the Lord will not be put to shame (Rom. 9.33; 10.11). Hays thus suggests that the mention of 'not being ashamed' would evoke such texts as Isaiah 50.7–8 (LXX), which declares: 'I know that I shall not be ashamed, because the one who justifies me is near.' So even before we reach the explicit quotation of Habakkuk 2.4, Paul has evoked a set of words and ideas (echoes) that provide the context (echo chamber) for understanding what comes next.

> Paul's allusive manner of using Scripture leaves enough silence for the voice of Scripture to answer back. Rather than filling the intertextual space with explanations, Paul encourages the reader to listen to more of Scripture's message than he himself voices. The word that Scripture speaks where Paul falls silent is a word that still has the power to contend against him.[4]

Such an approach allows us to appreciate Paul's use of Scripture in those letters that do not contain explicit quotations. For example, when faced with the possibility of execution, Paul says in Philippians 1.19: 'for I know that through your prayers and the help of the Spirit of Jesus Christ this will turn out [*apobesetai eis*] for my [*moi*] deliverance [*soterian*]'. This is perfectly understandable without thinking of the Old Testament, but the Greek of the last phrase is quite distinctive. The verb, which only occurs four times in the New Testament, literally means 'to disembark' (Luke 5.2; John 21.9), but when used with the preposition *eis* ('into') can mean 'end up' or 'turn out' (Luke 21.13; Phil. 1.19). The verb occurs 20 times in the LXX, 15 of which are in the book of Job. This itself is interesting, but more significantly, in Job 13.16 it occurs with the same noun (*soterian*) and pronoun (*moi*) as in Philippians 1.19. Hays writes:

> By echoing Job's words, Paul the prisoner tacitly assumes the role of righteous sufferer, as paradigmatically figured by Job. Awaiting trial, he speaks with Job's voice to affirm confidence in the favorable outcome of his afflictions; thereby he implicitly transfers to himself some of the significations that traditionally cluster about the figure of Job.[5]

Paul is not suggesting that his suffering is in any sense a 'fulfilment' of the Job passage. Rather, the echo sets up a link that invites comparison. In terms of similarities, Hays notes that Job's pain is compounded by the pious advice of his own friends, just as Paul's imprisonment is compounded by those who preach Christ out of envy (Phil. 1.15–17). As Hays says, 'The echo whispers a suggestion that the rival preachers have assumed the mantle of Job's hollow comforters; the falsehood of both will be exposed ultimately in the judgment of God.'[6] On the other hand, Paul is able to rejoice in his sufferings in a way Job could not, because he is clear that God is on his side. Paul possesses what Job lacked, namely the security of knowing that his suffering is in the service of Christ. Hence 'whereas Job, seeing through a glass darkly, endured his suffering with obdurate puzzlement, Paul, suffering as an apostle of Christ, interprets his suffering as a participation in the sufferings of the crucified Christ and thus finds himself able to rejoice in the midst of adversity'.[7]

Criteria for assessing the presence of an allusion

An obvious danger of an intertextual approach is discovering all manner of allusions and echoes that never entered Paul's mind. To combat this, Hays offers seven criteria by which we might test the legitimacy of any particular allusion or echo:

1 Availability: could Paul have known the text?
2 Volume: are there sufficient words in common and are they distinctive?
3 Recurrence: does Paul cite the text elsewhere?
4 Thematic coherence: does it fit Paul's argument?
5 Historical plausibility: is this suggestion consistent with what we know about Paul?
6 History of interpretation: has it been noticed before?
7 Satisfaction: does it lead to an insightful reading of the text?

These criteria are regularly cited by scholars in order to defend – or reject – a particular proposal, and have been subject to much debate. Michael Thompson, for example, uses 11 criteria to detect Gospel traditions in Romans 12.1—15.13, and Hays himself has refined the criteria in a later publication. Nevertheless, Hays asserts that despite:

> all the careful hedges that we plant around texts, meaning has a way of leaping over, like sparks. Texts are not inert; they burn and throw fragments of flame on their rising heat. Often we succeed in containing the energy, but sometimes the sparks escape and kindle new blazes, reprises of the original fire.[8]

Timothy Berkley

Berkley[9] draws on Hays's work but moves in a different direction. Hays frequently argues that allusions and echoes can be just as important for understanding Paul's thought as his explicit quotations. Berkley agrees, but wishes to establish another category, which he calls 'reference texts'. These are the texts that have engaged Paul in serious reflection and exegesis and form the foundation of his arguments. However, they are largely hidden from view and have to be 'detected' – like allusions and echoes – by the application of various criteria. This has two important consequences. First, Berkley does not think the explicit quotations are generally reference texts (that is, sites of exegesis); rather, they are usually proof texts to crown an argument reached on other grounds. Second, even though reference texts lie below the surface and therefore have to be detected, they do not lead to a variety of literary effects, as has been argued for allusion and echo. Berkley thinks that they are in fact our clearest guide to Paul's intended meaning.[10]

For example, what has often puzzled commentators is how Paul can assume that Jewish teachers who claim to know God are invariably idolaters, thieves and adulterers (Rom. 2.17–24). Berkley thinks the answer lies in three passages (Jer. 7.9–11; 9.23–24; Ezek. 36.21–23, 26) that qualify as reference texts and lie behind Paul's assertion. Paul is not basing his accusations on empirical evidence, which is manifestly false, but believes that this is the verdict of Scripture.

First, the Jeremiah 7.9–11 passage explains how Paul can accuse those who think their relationship to God will protect them from judgement. Not only does Paul derive the sins of idolatry, theft and adultery from this passage, he also derives the accusation that such things are a slur on God's name. It is a text known to the early Church in connection with Jesus' protest against the temple (Mark 11.17 and parallels):

> Will you *steal*, murder, commit *adultery*, swear falsely, *make offerings to Baal*, and go after other gods that you have not known, and then come and stand before me in this house, *which is called by my name*, and say, 'We are safe!' – only to go on doing all these abominations? Has this house, *which is called by my name*, become a den of robbers in your sight?

Second, the accusation about misplaced 'boasting' (Rom. 2.17, 23) derives from Jeremiah 9.23–24, where the word occurs no fewer than five times. Berkley argues that this text meets his conditions for a reference text by common vocabulary, Paul's use of it elsewhere (1 Cor. 1.31; 2 Cor. 10.17) and the fact that both Paul and Jeremiah go on to contrast physical circumcision with circumcision of the heart:

> Thus says the LORD: Do not let the wise *boast* in their wisdom, do not let the mighty *boast* in their might, do not let the wealthy *boast* in their wealth; but let those who *boast boast* in this, that they understand and know me, that I am the LORD...days are surely coming, says the LORD, when I will attend to all those who are *circumcised* only in the foreskin... *For all these nations are uncircumcised*, and all the house of Israel is *uncircumcised in heart*.

Third, the accusation that God's name is 'profaned among the nations' comes from Ezekiel 36.21–23, 26 where the phrase occurs three times. This text qualifies as a reference text by common vocabulary, Paul's use elsewhere (2 Cor. 3.3), links with the Jeremiah passages ('my name', 'the nations') and the fact that both Ezekiel and Paul go on to contrast flesh and heart:

> But I had concern for *my holy name*, which the house of Israel had *profaned among the nations* to which they came. Therefore say to the house of Israel, Thus says the Lord GOD: It is not for your sake, O house of Israel, that I am about to act, but for the sake of *my holy name*, which you have *profaned among the nations* to which you came. I will sanctify my great name, which has been *profaned among the nations*, and which you have profaned among them; and *the nations* shall know that I am the LORD, says the Lord GOD, when through you I display my holiness before their eyes...A new heart I will give you, and a new spirit I will put within you; and I will remove from your body the heart of stone and give you a heart of flesh.

From this Berkley concludes that Paul can accuse Jewish teachers of idolatry, theft and adultery because he finds such accusations written in Scripture. It is not a charge based on observation or even on the principle that thoughts are as bad as deeds (Sermon on the Mount). Paul's confidence that the indictments are true is based on the fact that they stand written in Scripture. Berkley also thinks that this explains Paul's use of Isaiah 52.5 in Romans 2.24: 'The name of God is blasphemed among the Gentiles because of you.' As we saw in Chapter 5, the problem with using Isaiah 52.5 in this way is that the original text was not condemning Israel for her sin but expressing compassion for her piteous state. For Berkley, the solution is that Isaiah 52.5 is not a 'reference text' in the way that the above passages are. It is Ezekiel 36 that tells Paul that God's name is being profaned because of Jewish sin, and the verbal connections with the Jeremiah passages complete his case. The quotation of the LXX of Isaiah 52.5 is simply a convenient way to conclude his argument with a succinct scriptural statement. It is not the rationale for Paul's accusation.[11]

Narrative approaches

Tom Wright

Wright agrees with Hays that allusions and echoes have a part to play in Paul's use of Scripture, but thinks that this approach can be too fragmentary. What really influences Paul and his readers is that they read texts in the light of an overall narrative framework. Scripture tells a story and Paul believes that the story has been brought to a climax in the Christ-event. For Wright, the key to understanding this story is that Paul and his fellow Jews would have believed that Israel was still in exile. Though some Jews had physically returned to Palestine after the Babylonian conquest, the promises associated with the final chapters of Deuteronomy (and Isaiah 40—55) had not yet been realized. The 'construal' with which Paul is working is a form of covenant theology that views the Christ-event as both announcing and accomplishing the end of Israel's exile. Thus in Wright's discussion of Galatians 3, he thinks the references to blessing and curse from Deuteronomy refer to this covenant theology. Because of national disobedience (not necessarily every individual), Israel went into exile and though now physically back in Palestine, their subjugation under the Romans shows that they are still in exile and therefore under the curse of the law. This came to a climax when Christ died on a Roman cross and took upon himself Israel's curse. But Deuteronomy also envisages restoration (what Jeremiah calls new covenant), and this has been inaugurated in Christ's resurrection and the outpouring of the Spirit:

Because the Messiah represents Israel, he is able to take upon himself Israel's curse and exhaust it. Jesus dies as the King of the Jews, at the hands of the Romans whose oppression of Israel is the present, and climactic, form of the curse of exile itself…Christ, as the representative Messiah, has achieved a specific task, that of taking upon himself the curse which hung over Israel and which on the one hand prevented her from enjoying full membership of Abraham's family and thereby on the other hand prevented the blessing of Abraham from flowing out to the Gentiles.[12]

Ross Wagner

Wagner notes that there are more explicit quotations from Isaiah in Romans (about 18) than from any other Old Testament book: there are about 13 from Psalms, 9 from Genesis and 8 from Deuteronomy. Since half of the letter's 60 or so quotations occur in Romans 9—11 (an average of one quotation every three verses), this is the focus of Wagner's study. He concludes that Paul read Isaiah as a three-act play of rebellion, punishment and restoration, and that he 'locates himself and his fellow believers (Jew and Gentile) in the final act of the story, where heralds go forth with the good news that God has redeemed his people'.[13] This involves a two-fold strategy: first, Paul read prophecies of Israel's deliverance as prophecies of his own gospel and mission; second, Paul read texts that denounce Israel's idolatry and unfaithfulness as referring to Israel's current resistance to the gospel. Wagner is keen to demonstrate that this does not mean that Paul simply imposed this framework on to Isaiah, for in:

> claiming that God will be faithful to redeem all Israel, Paul does not lean on the isolated testimony of a few verses from Isaiah. Rather, he taps into a broad and deep stream of thought that is characteristic of Isaiah's vision – a stream of thought, moreover, that is shared by numerous other prophetic texts and that is kept vigorously alive in later Jewish literature. Paul could probably assume that many of his listeners in Rome would be familiar with the broad outlines of this widely diffused eschatological hope for God's coming to deliver his people and to establish his reign over the cosmos.[14]

Sylvia Keesmaat

Keesmaat[15] shows how the exodus tradition has influenced Paul's exegesis in Romans 8.18–39 (and also Galatians). She notes that the key themes in this passage are adoption, being led by the Spirit, crying out to God as father, suffering, gaining an inheritance and entering into glory. Now these are usually understood as benefits for the individual Christian, but the perspective changes when it is recognized that these are all key themes in the exodus story. The besetting sin of the wilderness generation was their desire to return to Egypt and slavery again. The Spirit-inspired Christians must not follow their example but enter into the promised inheritance. It is the exodus story that is governing the shape of Paul's argument as he exhorts them not to abandon the tradition, 'for their own experience of God in Christ Jesus is rooted in the whole story of Israel. Adam and Abraham explain their past, the exodus gives meaning to their present, the whole story provides hope for their future'.[16] Drawing on both Hays and Wright, she states that the 'intertextual matrix upon which Paul draws is not just a cluster of motifs and themes which jostled around with one another in the collective mind of first-century Judaism. This matrix is actually a larger story, told and retold in past remembrance and future hope to shape Israel's identity and future expectation'.[17]

Francis Watson

Watson's[18] is one of the most ambitious attempts to establish a narrative approach to Paul's use of Scripture. He notes that the argument of Galatians 3 depends on explicit quotations from Genesis, Leviticus and Deuteronomy, together with a reference to the giving of the law from Exodus. Watson has sought to show that these are not isolated proof texts but represent a 'broad complex of scriptural material', to which he now adds the comment that they come from the 'Torah's beginning, its middle and its end'.[19] Though the order that these references appear in Galatians is Genesis–Deuteronomy–Leviticus–Exodus, Watson claims that Galatians 3 clearly presents itself as an 'interpretation of the Torah, a construal of the shape and logic of its fivefold form'.[20]

This is important for Watson, for he does not agree with the 'New Perspective' attempt to harmonize Leviticus 18.5 with Genesis 15.6 and Habakkuk 2.4. His understanding of Paul's construal of the law is that the earlier conditional promises were overtaken by the reality of sin and curse. Paul states this quite clearly in his interpretative remark, 'But the law is not of faith'. This is not to be regarded as Paul's imposition on the text, for he finds this antithesis in Scripture itself, the latter chapters of Deuteronomy being at odds with the earlier conditional promises:

> Paul practises a consecutive reading of his texts from Leviticus and Deuteronomy, in which the latter effectively cancels out the former. In doing so, he identifies a severe internal tension within the crucial closing chapters of Deuteronomy: the tension between conditional statements, which imply that the choice between blessing and curse, life and death is genuinely open, and statements of prophetic denunciation, in which the realization of the curse has become a certainty.[21]

Rhetorical approaches

Christopher Stanley

Stanley[22] challenges such 'maximal' interpretations of Paul's use of Scripture by appealing to the relatively low levels of literacy present in the first century and thus likely to be present in Paul's congregations. He accuses scholars of referring to the LXX as if it were a single book that one could take down off the shelf and use at will. The reality in the first century is that there was no such collection. There were individual scrolls but these were expensive to produce and very few of Paul's congregations would have been able to read them. Citing the work of Harris[23] and Gamble,[24] Stanley concludes that 'not more than a few individuals in Paul's churches, those recruited from the educated elite, would have been capable of reading and studying the Scriptures for themselves'.[25] This makes it highly unlikely that the majority of Christians would 'hear' the allusions and echoes that scholars such as Hays and Wagner propose. Indeed, with the possible exception of a few well-known scriptural events (creation, fall, exodus, conquest, exile) and people (Adam, Abraham, Moses, David) it would be almost impossible for the congregation to *know* the surrounding context of Paul's references, even if they are marked by a quotation formula (which allusions and echoes are not). Stanley therefore proposes a method whereby he will gauge how three different types of readers (or hearers) would most likely have understood Paul's quotations. He defines them as follows:

- An *informed audience* – those who would know the original context of every one of Paul's quotations and be willing to engage in critical dialogue with him.

- A *competent audience* – those who know the broad outline of the Scriptures but would not know the precise location of Paul's quotations.
- A *minimal audience* – those with little knowledge of the Scriptures but would perhaps appreciate/admire those like Paul who appear to be skilled in them.

When applied to the quotation of Isaiah 52.5 in Romans 2.24, Stanley thinks the *informed audience* would have considered the original context of Isaiah 52.5 and 'found themselves more confused than helped'.[26] They would immediately notice that the emphasis of the passage is deliverance not judgement and thus contrary to Paul's argument. They would see what most commentators have seen, namely that God's name is blasphemed because of the piteous state of Israel, leading them to 'question the entire premise of Paul's argument'.[27] The suggestion that Paul is reading Isaiah 52.5 through the lens of other texts such as Ezekiel 36 is dismissed with the words: 'How could Paul have expected the Romans to know this in the absence of any explicit reference?'[28] For Stanley, not even an *informed audience* could rise to this level of sophistication.

The *competent audience* would have been saved from these problems as they would not have known the original context of the quotation. They would assume, as no doubt the majority of Christians do today, that it means what Paul says it means. Hypocritical Jews, like those denounced in Romans 2.21–23, give God a bad name, as Scripture declares. Thus although the quotation does not support Paul's eventual conclusion that 'Jews as a class stand alongside Gentiles as the objects of God's threatened Judgment', it does offer strong support for the 'more limited indictment in 2:17–23 of Jews who hypocritically neglect their covenantal obligations'.[29]

The *minimal audience* would be much the same. They would have no way of knowing the context of Isaiah 52.5 or even where the quotation comes from. They would perhaps be impressed by Paul's ability to find quotations that support his argument, especially as it lays the foundation for his discussion of 'true' and 'false' Jews in the next section. Stanley suggests that since Paul could not rely on his apostolic authority to a church he had never visited, his mastery of the Scriptures would enhance his stature among the Romans and increase their openness to his argument.

The conclusion to be drawn from this is that Paul would hardly have based his arguments on what would have been inaccessible to his hearers/readers, or indeed would have been positively unhelpful. Rather, the focus of a study of Paul's use of Scripture should be on those things to which Paul draws the attention of his readers/hearers in order to make his point.

John Paul Heil

Heil[30] focuses on what Paul does to persuade his readers to accept his point of view. So while Hays and others look to the backgrounds of Isaiah 25.8 and Hosea 13.14 to explain Paul's combined quotation in 1 Corinthians 15.54–55 ('Death has been swallowed up in victory.' 'Where, O death, is your victory? Where, O death, is your sting?'), Heil notes that Paul introduces them as a single quotation ('then *the saying* that is written will be fulfilled'). Thus the readers/hearers 'need not recall the original source or context of either quotation, but merely accept the combination as a single prophecy from scripture yet to be fulfilled...Paul is relying upon his audience's recognition of scriptural authority *in general*'.[31]

Heil then describes the changes Paul has most likely made to the quotations in forming his composite quotation, but notes that this would have been hidden from his readers/hearers. They would simply hear a 'saying' that predicts the future conquest of death along with a taunt: 'Where, O death, is your victory?' The taunt is particularly apt since death's final victory over every human being is a universal theme in literature, theatre and proverbial wisdom. Paul's point is that in the resurrection of Christ death has been conquered, and it is his followers who have the final victory. There is no suggestion in any of this that the readers/hearers need to go in search of LXX scrolls in order to ascertain Paul's meaning. The composite quotation and the modifications Paul has made to the wording make it clear how he wants them to understand it. As with Stanley, Heil does not think that Paul has left the effectiveness of his arguments *conditional* on knowledge of the original contexts. The proper object of study is what Paul does with Scripture in order to persuade his readers/hearers to accept his arguments.[32]

Relevance theory

The relevance theory of Sperber and Wilson[33] may have much to offer in these debates. They advance the principle that 'relevance' is a key criterion for explaining the human activity of communication and cognition, that is, interpretation. It is true that readers of texts are confronted with a variety of factors that influence interpretation, but they will generally choose those that appear to be most relevant; that is, those that require least processing effort. Therefore if the composite quotation of Isaiah 25.8/Hosea 13.14 adequately explains Paul's point, there is no 'catalyst' to prompt a search for other meanings. On the other hand, if a particular quotation leads to some instability (it can't mean what it seems to mean), then the 'least processing effort' might be to seek a solution by digging out the original texts. The theory has been applied to the use of Scripture in the book of Revelation (Pattemore[34]) and will probably play a part in studies of Paul's use of Scripture in due course.

Conclusion

The study of Paul's use of Scripture received a fresh impetus with the discovery of the Dead Sea Scrolls (1947–). Here was a community like the early Church that not only saw itself as the fulfilment of the scriptural promises but also *claimed* fulfilment of texts that were not previously thought of as prophecies. Not all of its techniques can be found in Paul, but we have seen examples of allegory (Sarah and Hagar), typology (wilderness rebellions), merging quotations (Isa. 25.8; Hos. 13.14), use of variant texts ('Where, O death, is your *victory*'), changing the wording of texts ('her who was not beloved') and exploiting grammatical details (singular 'seed'). Although Paul could have got some of these things from his Greek background (a subject in need of further research), most scholars have found the parallels with the Dead Sea Scrolls illuminating.

A second impetus came with Hays's 1989 book, discussed above, on intertextual echo. Though Paul is not writing poetry, his careful use of allusion and echo can be analysed by applying the literary theories of such people as John Hollander and Thomas Greene.[35] Many scholars have embraced this, writing books and articles that explain a particular passage by reference either to neighbouring verses or similarly worded verses. The exception has been people like Stanley and Heil, who argue that Paul would not have made his point *dependent* on knowledge that was unlikely to be available to his hearers/readers. But even if this point is acknowledged, some would still argue that an intertextual approach is valuable for understanding *how* Paul arrived at his conclusions, even if he does not show his working (to use an examination phrase).

It is of course true that one's overall view of Scripture is bound to have an effect on how one analyses Paul's use of it, especially when a range of explanations are possible. For example, some scholars will wish to defend Paul from the accusation of changing the wording of texts and quoting them out of context. This is often done by drawing on the fact that the Dead Sea Scrolls have shown us that the biblical text existed in a variety of forms in the first century, and thus it is possible that Paul was quoting a *more original* form of the text than that which has come down to us, rather than changing the text. In addition it can be argued that Paul's quotations are not out of context if the neighbouring verses are taken into account, or the narrative framework to which it belongs. Behind such interpretative strategies often lies the question of whether Paul's use of Scripture offers a model for how Christians should use it today, and clearly many churches will not want their congregations changing the wording of Scripture and taking it out of context.[36]

On the other hand, other scholars point out that there is a huge difference between the cultural values of the first century and the modern world. It is therefore to be expected that Paul does things with texts that were considered legitimate (and persuasive) at the time but would not necessarily be so today. They would argue that there is no reason why we should 'defend' Paul from this and attempt to turn him into a modern historical-critical exegete. They would also cite the Dead Sea Scrolls, but to show how Paul's contemporaries were not constrained by the original meaning of the texts and routinely applied them to later events and people. Indeed, certain types of literary theory can be used to show that the meaning of texts is always 'potential' and only becomes 'concrete' when an actual reader attempts to interpret it. This is why it was 'obvious' to Paul that Scripture spoke about the Church, and 'obvious' to the Qumran community that it spoke about them. They both drew on the 'semantic potential' of texts to transcend their original contexts. Those who would espouse this view argue that modern-day Christians can learn from how Paul argued in his context, but should not attempt to reproduce it.[37]

Paul's use of Scripture remains a vibrant area of study today, whatever the particular standpoint of the scholar, and new books and articles emerge all the time. It is hoped that this book has both laid a foundation and stimulated an interest to go on and read further. To that end the reader's attention is drawn to the Select Bibliography provided below.

Appendix 1
Paul's quotations from Isaiah

No two languages have precise verbal equivalents, and so some variation between the Hebrew Scriptures (MT) and their Greek translation (LXX) is to be expected. However, this does not account for the sheer number and type of differences seen in the chart below (represented by italics). Out of 23 Isaiah quotations in Paul, only four can be said to be literal translations (no italics). About a dozen have either additional words (29.9–10, 14; 53.1; 65.2) or significantly different words (1.9; 28.11, 16; 40.13; 49.8; 52.11; 59.7; 64.4), while in six (8.14; 10.22–23; 11.10; 25.8; 52.5, 7) the meaning of the whole verse is different. This could be because the LXX translator misunderstood the Hebrew, didn't like the meaning of the Hebrew or was using a different Hebrew text from that which has come down to us. Alternatively, it could be that the LXX text represented by NETS is a revision of the original LXX, though the tendency of later versions was to bring it closer to the Hebrew. Most scholars believe they can detect examples of all these explanations in the Isaiah quotations on the following pages.

OT verse	NT verse	NRSV	NETS
Isa. 1.9	Rom. 9.29	If the Lord of hosts had not left us a few survivors, we would have been like Sodom, and become like Gomorrah.	And if the Lord Sabaoth had not left us *offspring*, we would have become like Sodoma and been made similar to Gomorra.
Isa. 8.14	Rom. 9.33	He will become a sanctuary, a stone one strikes against; for both houses of Israel he will become a rock one stumbles over – a trap and a snare for the inhabitants of Jerusalem.	*If you trust in him*, he will become your holy precinct, and you will *not encounter* him as a stumbling caused by a stone nor as a fall caused by a rock, *but the house of Iakob* is in a trap, and those who sit in Ierousalem are in a pit.
Isa. 10.22–23	Rom. 9.27–28	For though your people Israel were like the sand of the sea, only a remnant of them will return. Destruction is decreed, overflowing with righteousness. For the Lord God of hosts will make a full end, as decreed, in all the earth.	And *if* the people of Israel *become* like the sand of the sea, the remnant will be saved, for he is completing and *cutting short* a reckoning with righteousness, because God will perform a *shortened reckoning* in the whole world.
Isa. 11.10	Rom. 15.12	On that day the root of Jesse shall stand as a signal to the peoples; the nations shall inquire of him, and his dwelling shall be glorious.	And there shall be on that day the root of Iessai, even the one who stands up to *rule* nations; nations shall *hope* in him, and his rest shall be honor.
Isa. 22.13	1 Cor. 15.32	'Let us eat and drink, for tomorrow we die.'	Let us eat and drink, for tomorrow we die.
Isa. 25.8	1 Cor. 15.54	He will swallow up death for ever.	*Death, having prevailed, swallowed them up* …

OT verse	NT verse	NRSV	NETS
Isa. 27.9	Rom. 11.27	Therefore by this the guilt of Jacob will be expiated, and this will be the full fruit of the removal of his sin…	Because of this the lawlessness of Iakob will be removed. And this is his blessing, when I remove his sin…
Isa. 28.11	1 Cor. 14.21	Truly, with stammering lip and with alien tongue he will speak to this people…	because of *contempt* from lips, through a different tongue, because *they* will speak to this people…
Isa. 28.16	Rom. 9.33; 10.11	See, I am laying in Zion a foundation stone, a tested stone, a precious cornerstone, a sure foundation: 'One who trusts will not panic.'	See, I *will* lay for the foundations of Sion a precious, choice stone, a highly valued cornerstone for its foundations, and the one who believes *in him will not be put to shame*.
Isa. 29.9–10	Rom. 11.8	Stupefy yourselves and be in a stupor, blind yourselves and be blind! Be drunk, but not from wine; stagger, but not from strong drink! For the LORD has poured out upon you a spirit of deep sleep; he has closed your eyes, you prophets, and covered your heads, you seers.	Be faint and amazed; get a drunken headache – not from strong drink nor from wine! Because the Lord *has made you drink* with a spirit of deep sleep; *he will* close their eyes and those of their prophets *and of their rulers* – the ones who see the *hidden things*.
Isa. 29.14	1 Cor. 1.19	I will again do amazing things with this people, shocking and amazing. The wisdom of their wise shall perish, and the discernment of the discerning shall be hidden.	Therefore look, I will proceed to *remove* this people. I will *remove them* and destroy the wisdom of the wise, and the discernment of the discerning I will hide.
Isa. 40.13; 1 Cor. 2.16	Rom. 11.34; 1 Cor. 2.16	Who has directed the spirit of the LORD, or as his counsellor has instructed him?	Who has *known the mind* of the Lord, and who has been his counselor to instruct him?

Isa. 49.8	2 Cor. 6.2	Thus says the LORD: In a time of favour I have answered you, on a day of salvation I have helped you…	Thus says the Lord: In an acceptable time I have *listened* to you, on a day of salvation I have helped you…
Isa. 52.5	Rom. 2.24	Their rulers howl, says the LORD, and continually, all day long, my name is despised.	This is what the Lord says, *Because of you,* my name is continually blasphemed *among the nations.*
Isa. 52.7	Rom. 10.15	How beautiful upon the mountains are the feet of the messenger who announces peace, who brings good news, who announces salvation, who says to Zion, 'Your God reigns.'	*I am here, like season* upon the mountains, like the feet of one bringing glad tidings of a *report* of peace, like one bringing glad tidings *of good things, because I will make* your salvation heard, saying to Sion, 'Your God shall reign'.
Isa. 52.11	2 Cor. 6.17	Depart, depart, go out from there! Touch no unclean thing; go out from the midst of it, purify yourselves…	Depart, depart, go out from there, and touch no unclean thing; go out from the midst of it; *be separated…*
Isa. 52.15	Rom. 15.21	so he shall startle many nations; kings shall shut their mouths because of him; for that which had not been told them they shall see, and that which they had not heard they shall contemplate.	so shall many nations be astonished at him, and kings shall shut their mouth, because those who were not informed about him shall see and those who did not hear shall understand.
Isa. 53.1	Rom. 10.16	Who has believed what we have heard?	*Lord,* who has believed our report?
Isa. 54.1	Gal. 4.27	Sing, O barren one who did not bear; burst into song and shout, you who have not been in labour! For the children of the desolate woman will be more than the children of her that is married…	Rejoice, O barren one who does not bear; break forth, and shout, you who are not in labor! Because more are the children of the desolate woman than of her that has a husband…

OT verse	NT verse	NRSV	NETS
Isa. 59.7–8	Rom. 3.15–17	Their feet run to evil, and they rush to shed innocent blood; their thoughts are thoughts of iniquity, desolation and destruction are in their highways. The way of peace they do not know…	And their feet run to evil, swift to shed blood, and their reasonings are reasonings of *fools*; destruction and wretchedness are in their ways. And a way of peace they do not know…
Isa. 59.20–21	Rom. 11.26–27	And he will come to Zion as Redeemer, to those in Jacob who turn from transgression, says the LORD. And as for me, this is my covenant with them, says the LORD…	And the one who delivers will come for Sion's sake, *and he will turn* impiety away from Iakob. And this is the covenant to them from me, said the Lord…
Isa. 64.4	1 Cor. 2.9	From ages past no one has heard, no ear has perceived, no eye has seen any God besides you, who works for those who wait for him.	From ages past *we* have not heard, nor have *our* eyes seen any God beside you, and your works, which you will do to those who wait *for mercy*.
Isa. 65.1–2	Rom. 10.20–21	I was ready to be sought out by those who did not ask, to be found by those who did not seek me. I said, 'Here I am, here I am', to a nation that did not call on my name. I held out my hands all day long to a rebellious people, who walk in a way that is not good, following their own devices…	I became visible to those who were not seeking me; I was found by those who were not inquiring about me. I said, 'Here I am', to the nation that did not call my name. I stretched out my hands all day long to a disobedient *and contrary* people, who did not walk in a true way but after their own sins.

Appendix 2

Index of Paul's quotations

Gen. 2.7	1 Cor. 15.45	Deut. 30.12–14	Rom. 10.6–8
Gen. 2.24	1 Cor. 6.16; Eph. 5.31	Deut. 32.21	Rom. 10.19
Gen. 12.3	Gal. 3.8	Deut. 32.35	Rom. 12.19
Gen. 12.7	Gal. 3.16	Deut. 32.43	Rom. 15.10
Gen. 15.5	Rom. 4.18		
Gen. 15.6	Rom. 4.3, 9, 22; Gal. 3.6	2 Sam. 7.8, 14	2 Cor. 6.18
Gen. 17.5	Rom. 4.17, 18		
Gen. 18.10, 14	Rom. 9.9	1 Kings 19.10, 14	Rom. 11.3
Gen. 18.18	Gal. 3.8	1 Kings 19.18	Rom. 11.4
Gen. 21.10	Gal. 4.30		
Gen. 21.12	Rom. 9.7	Job 5.13	1 Cor. 3.19
Gen. 25.23	Rom. 9.12	Job 41.11	Rom. 11.35
Exod. 9.16	Rom. 9.17	Ps. 4.4	Eph. 4.26
Exod. 16.18	2 Cor. 8.15	Ps. 5.9	Rom. 3.13
Exod. 20.12	Eph. 6.2–3	Ps. 8.6	1 Cor. 15.27
Exod. 20.13–17	Rom. 13.9	Ps. 10.7	Rom. 3.14
Exod. 20.17	Rom. 7.7	Ps. 14.1–3	Rom. 3.10–12
Exod. 32.6	1 Cor. 10.7	Ps. 18.49	Rom. 15.9
Exod. 33.19	Rom. 9.15	Ps. 19.4	Rom. 10.18
		Ps. 24.1	1 Cor. 10.26
Lev. 18.5	Rom. 10.5; Gal. 3.12	Ps. 32.1–2	Rom. 4.7–8
Lev. 19.18	Rom. 13.9; Gal. 5.14	Ps. 36.1	Rom. 3.18
Lev. 26.12	2 Cor. 6.16	Ps. 44.22	Rom. 8.36
		Ps. 51.4	Rom. 3.4
Num. 16.5	2 Tim. 2.19	Ps. 68.18	Eph. 4.8
		Ps. 69.9	Rom. 15.3
Deut. 5.16	Eph. 6.2–3	Ps. 69.22–23	Rom. 11.9–10
Deut. 5.17–21	Rom. 13.9	Ps. 94.11	1 Cor. 3.20
Deut. 5.21	Rom. 7.7	Ps. 112.9	2 Cor. 9.9
Deut. 9.4	Rom. 10.6	Ps. 116.10	2 Cor. 4.13
Deut. 17.7	1 Cor. 5.13	Ps. 117.1	Rom. 15.11
Deut. 19.15	2 Cor. 13.1		
Deut. 21.23	Gal. 3.13	Prov. 25.21–22	Rom. 12.20
Deut. 25.4	1 Cor. 9.9; 1 Tim. 5.18		
Deut. 27.26	Gal. 3.10	Isa. 1.9	Rom. 9.29
Deut. 29.4	Rom. 11.8	Isa. 8.14	Rom. 9.33

Appendix 2

Isa. 10.22–23	Rom. 9.27–28	Isa. 59.20–21	Rom. 11.26–27
Isa. 11.10	Rom. 15.12	Isa. 64.4	1 Cor. 2.9
Isa. 22.13	1 Cor. 15.32	Isa. 65.1–2	Rom. 10.20–21
Isa. 25.8	1 Cor. 15.54		
Isa. 27.9	Rom. 11.27	Jer. 9.24	1 Cor. 1.31; 2 Cor. 10.17
Isa. 28.11–12	1 Cor. 14.21		
Isa. 28.16	Rom. 9.33; 10.11	Ezek. 20.34, 31	2 Cor. 6.17
Isa. 29.10	Rom. 11.8	Ezek. 37.27	2 Cor. 6.16
Isa. 29.14	1 Cor. 1.19		
Isa. 40.13	Rom. 11.34; 1 Cor. 2.16	Hos. 1.10	Rom. 9.26
Isa. 45.23	Rom. 14.11	Hos. 2.23	Rom. 9.25
Isa. 49.8	2 Cor. 6.2	Hos. 13.14	1 Cor. 15.55
Isa. 52.5	Rom. 2.24		
Isa. 52.7	Rom. 10.15	Joel 2.32	Rom. 10.13
Isa. 52.15	Rom. 15.21		
Isa. 53.1	Rom. 10.16	Hab. 2.4	Rom. 1.17; Gal. 3.11
Isa. 54.1	Gal. 4.27		
Isa. 59.7–8	Rom. 3.15–17	Mal. 1.2–3	Rom. 9.13

Appendix 3
Extracts from the Dead Sea Scrolls

The following extracts are taken from the edition of Geza Vermes, *The Complete Dead Sea Scrolls in English* (London: Penguin, 1997). The biblical text that is being commented on is printed in italics. Square brackets represent text that is missing from the scroll (because of its fragmentary nature) and that has been reconstructed to fit the length of the gap.

1 The Habakkuk commentary (1QpHab)

And the Lord answered [and said to me, 'Write down the vision and make it plain] upon the tablets, that [he who reads] may read it speedily… and God told Habakkuk to write down that which would happen to the final generation, but He did not make known to him when time would come to an end. And as for that which He said, *That he who reads may read it speedily:* interpreted this concerns the Teacher of Righteousness, to whom God made known all the mysteries of the words of His servants the Prophets. *For there shall be yet another vision concerning the appointed time. It shall tell of the end and shall not lie.* Interpreted, this means that the final age shall be prolonged, and shall exceed all that the Prophets have said; for the mysteries of God are astounding. *If it tarries, wait for it, for it shall surely come and shall not be late.* Interpreted, this concerns the men of truth who keep the Law, whose hands shall not slacken in the service of truth when the final age is prolonged. For all the ages of God reach their appointed end as he determines for them in the mysteries of His wisdom. *Behold, [his soul] is puffed up and is not right.* Interpreted, this means that [the wicked] shall double their guilt upon themselves [and it shall not be forgiven] when they are judged…[*But the righteous shall live by his faith*]. Interpreted, this concerns all those who observe the Law in the House of Judah, whom God will deliver from the House of Judgement because of their suffering and because of their faith in the Teacher of Righteousness. (1QpHab 6.12—7.5)

2 The Florilegium (4Q174)

The Lord declares to you that He will build you a House. I will raise up your seed after you. I will establish the throne of his kingdom [for ever]. I [will be] his father and he shall be my son. He is the Branch of David who shall arise with the Interpreter of the Law [to rule] in Zion [at the end] of time. As it is written, *I will raise up the tent of David that is fallen.* That is to say, the fallen *tent of David* is he who shall arise to save Israel...*[Why] do the nations rage...[and the] princes take counsel together against the Lord and against [His Messiah]?* Interpreted, this saying concerns [the kings of the nations]...This is the time of which it is written in the book of Daniel, the prophet: *But the wicked shall do wickedly and shall not understand, but the righteous shall purify themselves and make themselves white.* (4Q174 1.10–13, 18–19; 2.1–3)

3 The Hymn Scroll (1QH)

They caused [me] to be like a ship on the deeps of the [sea], and like a fortified city before [the aggressor], [and] like a woman in travail with her first-born child, upon whose belly pangs have come and grievous pains, filling with anguish her child-bearing crucible. For the children have come to the throes of Death, and she labours in her pains who bears a man. For amid the throes of Death she shall bring forth a man-child, and amid the pains of Hell there shall spring from her child-bearing crucible a Marvellous Mighty Counsellor; and a man shall be delivered from out of the throes. (1QH Hymn 4)

4 The Damascus Document (CD)

I will exile the tabernacle of your king and the bases of your statues from my tent to Damascus. The Books of the Law are the *tabernacle of the king*; as God said, *I will raise up the tabernacle of David which is fallen.* The *king* is the congregation; and the *bases of the statues* are the books of the Prophets whose sayings Israel despised. The *star* is the Interpreter of the Law who shall come to Damascus; as it is written, *A star shall come forth out of Jacob and a sceptre shall rise out of Israel.* (CD 7.14–21)

Notes

Introduction

1 K. Stendahl, *Paul among Jews and Gentiles* (Philadelphia: Fortress Press, 1976).
2 A. Pietersma and B. G. Wright (eds), *New English Translation of the Septuagint* (New York: Oxford University Press, 2007).

1 Paul and the creation stories

1 *Heres* 56–57, quoted in J. D. G. Dunn, *The Theology of Paul the Apostle* (Edinburgh: T. & T. Clark, 1998), p. 87.
2 See N. T. Wright, *The Climax of the Covenant: Christ and the Law in Pauline Theology* (Edinburgh: T. & T. Clark, 1991), pp. 18–40.
3 Dunn, *Theology of Paul the Apostle*, pp. 281–7.

2 Paul and Abraham

1 For a lucid introduction to Paul's understanding of these ideas, see J. M. Bassler, *Navigating Paul: An Introduction to Key Theological Concepts* (Louisville, KY: Westminster John Knox, 2006).
2 R. B. Hays, *Echoes of Scripture in the Letters of Paul* (New Haven, CT: Yale University Press, 1989), pp. 154–92.
3 N. T. Wright, *The Climax of the Covenant: Christ and the Law in Pauline Theology* (Edinburgh: T. & T. Clark, 1991), pp. 157–74.

3 Paul and Moses

1 See the dictionary article on 'Moses' by J. Jeremias in vol. 4 of the *Theological Dictionary of the New Testament* (Grand Rapids, MI: Eerdmans, 1967), pp. 848–73. The quotation is from p. 849.
2 S. J. Hafemann, *Paul, Moses, and the History of Israel: The Letter/Spirit Contrast and the Argument from Scripture in 2 Corinthians 3* (Carlisle: Paternoster, 2005), pp. 63–91.
3 R. B. Hays, *Echoes of Scripture in the Letters of Paul* (New Haven, CT: Yale University Press, 1989), p. 107.
4 E.g. 'the Jews were entrusted with the oracles of God' (Rom. 3.3); 'we uphold the law' (Rom. 3.31); 'we know that the law is spiritual' (Rom. 7.14). See J. W. Drane, *Paul: Libertine or Legalist?* (London: SPCK, 1975), p. 34.

5 The standard work is L. Goppelt, *Typos: The Typological Interpretation of the Old Testament in the New* (Grand Rapids, MI: Eerdmans, 1982). See also J. Whitman, *Interpretation and Allegory: Antiquity to the Modern Period* (Leiden: Brill, 2000) and F. W. Young, *Biblical Exegesis and the Formation of Christian Culture* (Cambridge: Cambridge University Press, 1997).

6 Hays, *Echoes of Scripture*, p. 105.

7 A. T. Hanson, *Studies in Paul's Technique and Theology* (London: SPCK, 1974).

8 *Sukkah* 3.11, quoted in F. C. Holmgren, *The Old Testament and the Significance of Jesus* (Grand Rapids, MI: Eerdmans, 1999), p. 32.

9 Strangely, the majority of manuscripts read 'written on *our* hearts', which fits uneasily with their role as testimony 'to be known and read by all'. A few mss (‭א‬ 33 1175 1881 pc) read 'your', and this was the reading adopted by the RSV.

10 F. Adeyemi, *The New Covenant Torah in Jeremiah and the Law of Christ in Paul* (Frankfurt am Main: Peter Lang, 2006). There have been a number of important studies on 2 Corinthians 3. See L. L. Belleville, *Reflections of Glory: Paul's Polemical Use of the Moses–Doxa Tradition in 2 Corinthians 3.1–18* (Sheffield: JSOT Press, 1991); N. T. Wright, *The Climax of the Covenant: Christ and the Law in Pauline Theology* (Edinburgh: T. & T. Clark, 1991), pp. 175–92; Hays, *Echoes of Scripture*, pp. 122–53.

11 F. Watson, *Paul and the Hermeneutics of Faith* (London: T. & T. Clark, 2004), pp. 297–8.

12 E. E. Ellis, *Paul's Use of the Old Testament* (Edinburgh: Oliver & Boyd, 1957), p. 145. For an introduction to the Dead Sea Scrolls, see H. Stegemann, *The Library of Qumran* (Grand Rapids, MI: Eerdmans, 1998).

4 Paul and the law

1 R. Bultmann, *Theology of the New Testament*, vol. 1 (London: SCM, 1952).

2 E. P. Sanders, *Paul and Palestinian Judaism* (London: SCM, 1977).

3 First in his article, J. D. G. Dunn, 'The New Perspective on Paul', *Bulletin of the John Rylands Library* 65 (1983), 95–122, and in more detail in *The Theology of Paul the Apostle* (Edinburgh: T. & T. Clark, 1998), pp. 334–89.

4 At the time of writing, the website 'The Paul Page' lists hundreds of articles from New Perspective scholars, as well as defences of the Reformation view.

5 J. R. Wagner, *Heralds of the Good News: Isaiah and Paul 'In Concert' in the Letter to the Romans* (Leiden: Brill, 2002), p. 167.

6 Wagner, *Heralds of the Good News*, p. 201.

7 R. B. Hays, *The Faith of Jesus Christ: An Investigation of the Narrative Substructure of Galatians 3:1—4:11* (SBLDS 56; Chico, CA: Scholars Press, 1983).

8 In the second edition of his work (Eerdmans, 2002), Hays lists an impressive list of scholars who now adopt this interpretation. James Dunn, however, is not one of them, and Hays includes his critique of it as an appendix to his book. The suggestion that Paul read Habakkuk 2.4 as a reference to the messiah was made by A. T. Hanson, *Studies in Paul's Technique and Theology* (London: SPCK, 1974), pp. 39–45. The argument is based on evidence that 'The Righteous One' was understood as a messianic title (Acts 3.14) and certain peculiarities of the LXX translation of Habakkuk 2.2–4, which can be read: 'If *he* delays, wait for *him*, because a Coming One will arrive.' The Hebrew is referring to the vision that is coming but the LXX has used a masculine pronoun, implying a person.

9 F. Watson, *Paul and the Hermeneutics of Faith* (London: T. & T. Clark, 2004), p. 520.

10 H. Hübner, *Law in Paul's Thought* (Edinburgh: T. & T. Clark, 1984).

11 H. Räisänen, *Paul and the Law* (Philadelphia: Fortress Press, 1986).

12 For a good exploration of these issues, see A. A. Das, *Paul, the Law and the Covenant* (Peabody: Hendrickson, 2001).

5 Paul and the prophets: Israel and the Gentiles

1 J. R. Wagner, *Heralds of the Good News: Isaiah and Paul 'In Concert' in the Letter to the Romans* (Leiden: Brill, 2002).

2 R. B. Hays, *Echoes of Scripture in the Letters of Paul* (New Haven, CT: Yale University Press, 1989), p. 63, draws attention to the fact that Paul appears to echo the language of the suffering servant (e.g. Rom. 4.24–25; 5.15–19; 10.16; 15.21), but whether through 'evasion or reticence' does not make explicit the 'prophetic typology that would supremely integrate his interpretation of Christ and Israel'. Seifrid argues that the 'report' mentioned in Isaiah 53.1 must represent the content of Isaiah 53 (i.e. the suffering servant) and that since Paul identifies this 'report' with his own proclamation of the gospel, he is implicitly identifying Christ with the figure of Isaiah 53. This is possible, but as with Hays, it remains noteworthy that Paul never makes this explicit. See M. D. Seifrid, 'Romans' in G. K. Beale and D. A. Carson (eds), *Commentary on the New Testament Use of the Old Testament* (Grand Rapids, MI: Baker, 2007), p. 663.

3 The NRSV has swopped the negatives to read: 'No one who believes in him will be put to shame.' Paul follows the LXX in using the verb 'to be ashamed' instead of the Hebrew 'to panic', though he uses the future passive instead of the LXX's aorist subjunctive.

4 Strazicich suggests that the LXX of Joel 2.32b might have prompted Paul to change the singular to a plural, since it rendered the Hebrew 'survivors' with 'heralds', possibly because it misread the Hebrew consonants *bsridim*

as *mbrsim*. See J. Strazicich, *Joel's Use of Scripture and the Scripture's Use of Joel: Appropriation and Resignification in Second Temple Judaism and Early Christianity* (Leiden: Brill, 2007), p. 323.

5 Hays, *Echoes of Scripture*, p. 67. As we shall see in Chapter 8, other commentators regard such 'poetic' explanations as obscuring the point that Paul has simply taken the text out of context. If the 'opaque original sense has vanished altogether', is this not just a fancy way of saying that he has substituted his own meaning for anything that was originally there?

6 Wagner, *Heralds of the Good News*, p. 212.

7 Wagner, *Heralds of the Good News*, p. 323.

8 See S. Moyise, *Evoking Scripture: Seeing the Old Testament in the New* (London and New York: T. & T. Clark, 2008), pp. 33–48.

9 The two Isaiah quotations carry the positive message that God has preserved a remnant. Isaiah 1.9 carries the realization that unless God 'had not left us a few survivors [LXX "seed"], we would have been like Sodom, and become like Gomorrah'. Isaiah 10.22–23 is more difficult, partly because of the meaning of v. 22b ('Destruction is decreed, overflowing with righteousness') and partly because of the awkward comparison in v. 22a (lit. 'Though your people Israel are like the sand of the sea a remnant will return'), which sounds as though Israel is currently numerous but about to be reduced. The majority of translations clarify the contrast by adding the word 'only' ('Though your people...only a remnant will return'). The NRSV puts the first clause in the past tense ('For though your people were like the sand of the sea, only...'), turning the contrast into a numerous past and a minority present, rather than a numerous present and a minority future.

10 J. R. Harris, *Testimonies* (Cambridge: Cambridge University Press, 2 vols, 1916, 1920); C. H. Dodd, *According to the Scriptures: The Sub-structure of New Testament Theology* (London: Nisbet, 1952). For a recent discussion of the evidence, see M. C. Albl, *'And Scripture Cannot be Broken': The Form and Function of Early Christian Testimonia Collections* (Leiden: Brill, 1999).

11 Wagner, *Heralds of the Good News*, p. 305.

6 Paul and the prophets: the life of the Christian community

1 In Hannah's song (1 Sam. 2.1–10), the LXX of verse 10 includes a sentence that is absent from the Hebrew text: 'Let not the wise man boast in his wisdom, nor let the mighty man boast in his strength, and let not the rich man boast in his wealth; but let him that boasts boast in this, to understand and know the Lord and to execute judgement and justice in the midst of the earth.' It is possible that Paul may also have this in mind.

2 Most scholars agree that Paul has changed the final word 'hidden' to 'thwart'. This gives a rhetorically powerful parallelism: 'I will destroy the wisdom of the wise/and the discernment of the discerning I will thwart.' As John Paul Heil says: 'This highly artistic, poetic, and concise chiasm makes the quotation memorable...and potently and poetically persuades its audience to turn away from worldly wisdom to the power of God' – J. P. Heil, *The Rhetorical Role of Scripture in 1 Corinthians* (Atlanta, GA: SBL, 2005), p. 22.

3 Paul omits what was said to this people ('This is rest; give rest to the weary; and this is repose') as this would obscure his point. He also changes the statement that they would not hear to a future prediction, 'they will not listen'. Heil thinks that Paul's introduction ('In the law it is written') indicates a general reference to Scripture rather than a specific reference to Isaiah, and may have other passages such as Deuteronomy 28.49 and Jeremiah 5.15 in mind. This can then account for the future tense. See Heil, *Rhetorical Role of Scripture*, pp. 191–203.

4 This is the only occurrence of the word in the New Testament. It may derive from the Hebrew expression *bene beliyyaal*, which means 'sons of worthlessness', but was rendered 'sons of Belial' in the KJV. It occurs in the Dead Sea Scrolls as the name of the prince of evil, which appears to be Paul's meaning here.

5 Once again, the manuscript tradition is confused, as we can see if we offer a literal translation of the Hebrew and Greek of Hosea 13.14. Hence the Hebrew: 'Where are your plagues, O death? Where is your destruction, O Sheol?'; and the LXX: 'Where is your judgement, O death? Where is your sting, O Hades?' It is possible that Paul is using an alternative Greek text that has not come down to us, though the view that Paul has added 'in victory' is more likely than the view that other Greek manuscripts included it in both Isaiah 25.8 and Hosea 13.14.

6 R. B. Hays, *Echoes of Scripture in the Letters of Paul* (New Haven, CT: Yale University Press, 1989), pp. 84–7. The subsequent debate can be found in C. A. Evans and J. A. Sanders (eds), *Paul and the Scriptures of Israel* (Sheffield: JSOT Press, 1993).

7 Paul and the writings

1 Also of note is the prologue to the book of Sirach (LXX) which says: 'Many great teachings have been given to us through the Law and the Prophets and the others that followed them.'

2 J. R. Wagner, *Heralds of the Good News: Isaiah and Paul 'In Concert' in the Letter to the Romans* (Leiden: Brill, 2002), p. 186.

3 A. T. Hanson, *Studies in Paul's Technique and Theology* (London: SPCK, 1974).

4 R. B. Hays, *The Conversion of the Imagination: Paul as Interpreter of Israel's Scripture* (Grand Rapids, MI: Eerdmans, 2005).

5 This is why Acts can quote Psalm 69.25 ('Let his homestead become desolate, and let there be no one to live in it') as a reference to the fate of Judas, even though the original says: lit. 'May their homestead become desolate, may no one live in their tents.'

6 Psalm 5.12 ('For you bless the righteous, O LORD; you cover them with favour as with a shield'); 10.17 ('O LORD, you will hear the desire of the meek; you will strengthen their heart...'); 36.10 ('O continue your steadfast love to those who know you, and your salvation to the upright of heart'); 140.12–13 ('I know that the LORD maintains the cause of the needy, and executes justice for the poor. Surely the righteous shall give thanks to your name').

7 J. D. G. Dunn, *Romans 1—8* (WBC 38; Dallas, TX: Word Books, 1988), pp. 149–51. He says that 'it needs to be stressed that the point of the catena is not simply to demonstrate that scripture condemns all human-kind, but more precisely to demonstrate that scriptures which had been read from the presupposition of a clear distinction between the righteous and the unrighteous...in fact condemned all humankind as soon as that clear distinction was undermined' (p. 149).

8 So S. C. Keesmaat, 'The Psalms in Romans and Galatians' in S. Moyise and M. J. J. Menken (eds), *The Psalms in the New Testament* (London and New York: T. & T. Clark, 2004), pp. 145–8.

9 See N. T. Wright, *The Climax of the Covenant: Christ and the Law in Pauline Theology* (Edinburgh: T. & T. Clark, 1991), pp. 26–34.

10 In a similar way the designation of someone as a 'son of man' in the Hebrew Bible is simply a poetic way of referring to their humanness and mortality (Ezek. 2.1; 3.1; 4.1 etc.). But in Daniel's vision, the 'one like a son of man', who will be given an everlasting dominion (7.14), is later identified with the 'holy ones of the Most High' who will gain 'possession of the kingdom'.

11 C. K. Barrett, *The Epistle to the Romans* (London: A. & C. Black, 1962), pp. 242–3.

12 G. Zerbe, 'Paul's Ethic of Nonretaliation and Peace' in W. M. Swartley (ed.), *The Love of Enemy and Nonretaliation in the New Testament* (Louisville, KY: Westminster John Knox, 1992), pp. 177–222.

8 Modern approaches to Paul's use of Scripture

1 R. B. Hays, *Echoes of Scripture in the Letters of Paul* (New Haven, CT: Yale University Press, 1989).

2 Translation by Hays.

3 Hays, *Echoes of Scripture*, p. 36. The influence of Psalm 98.2 on Romans 1.16–17 has been taken up by Douglas A. Campbell in his chapter, 'The

Meaning of *dikaiosyne theou* in Romans: An Intertextual suggestion' in S. E. Porter and C. D. Stanley (eds), *As it is Written: Studying Paul's Use of Scripture* (Atlanta, GA: SBL, 2008), pp. 189–212.

4 Hays, *Echoes of Scripture*, p. 177.

5 Hays, *Echoes of Scripture*, p. 22.

6 Hays, *Echoes of Scripture*, p. 23.

7 Hays, *Echoes of Scripture*, p. 22.

8 Hays, *Echoes of Scripture*, p. 33. See also M. B. Thompson, *Clothed with Christ: The Example and Teaching of Jesus in Romans 12.1—15.13* (JSNTSup 59; Sheffield: JSOT Press, 1991), pp. 30–7; and for a discussion of the criteria, S. E. Porter, 'Allusions and Echoes' in Porter and Stanley, *As it is Written*, pp. 29–40.

9 T. W. Berkley, *From a Broken Covenant to Circumcision of the Heart: Pauline Intertextual Exegesis in Romans 2.17–29* (SBLDS 175; Atlanta, GA: SBL, 2000).

10 This section draws on S. Moyise, *Evoking Scripture: Seeing the Old Testament in the New* (London and New York: T. & T. Clark, 2008), pp. 33–48.

11 I have offered a critique of this particular example in Moyise, *Evoking Scripture*, pp. 33–48.

12 N. T. Wright, *The Climax of the Covenant: Christ and the Law in Pauline Theology* (Edinburgh: T. & T. Clark, 1991), p. 151.

13 J. R. Wagner, *Heralds of the Good News: Isaiah and Paul 'In Concert' in the Letter to the Romans* (Leiden: Brill, 2002), p. 354.

14 Wagner, *Heralds of the Good News*, p. 297.

15 S. C. Keesmaat, *Paul and his Story: (Re)Interpreting the Exodus Tradition* (JSNTSup 181; Sheffield: Sheffield Academic Press, 1999).

16 Keesmaat, *Paul and his Story*, p. 227.

17 Keesmaat, *Paul and his Story*, p. 228.

18 F. Watson, *Paul and the Hermeneutics of Faith* (London: T. & T. Clark, 2004).

19 Watson, *Paul and the Hermeneutics of Faith*, p. 517.

20 Watson, *Paul and the Hermeneutics of Faith*, p. 517.

21 Watson, *Paul and the Hermeneutics of Faith*, p. 429.

22 C. D. Stanley, *Arguing with Scripture: The Rhetoric of Quotations in the Letters of Paul* (New York and London: T. & T. Clark, 2004).

23 W. Harris, *Ancient Literacy* (Cambridge, MA: Harvard University Press, 1989).

24 H. Y. Gamble, *Books and Readers in the Early Church: A History of Early Christian Texts* (New Haven, CT: Yale University Press, 1995).

25 Stanley, *Arguing with Scripture*, p. 45.

26 Stanley, *Arguing with Scripture*, p. 147.

27 Stanley, *Arguing with Scripture*, p. 148.
28 Stanley, *Arguing with Scripture*, p. 148, n. 30.
29 Stanley, *Arguing with Scripture*, p. 149.
30 J. P. Heil, *The Rhetorical Role of Scripture in 1 Corinthians* (Atlanta, GA: SBL, 2005).
31 Heil, *Rhetorical Role of Scripture*, pp. 247–8. Emphasis added.
32 For a rhetorical approach that focuses on allusions and echoes, see R. E. Ciampa, *The Presence and Function of Scripture in Galatians 1 and 2* (WUNT, 2.102; Tübingen: Mohr Siebeck, 1998).
33 D. Sperber and D. Wilson, *Relevance: Communication and Cognition* (2nd edn; Oxford: Blackwell, 1995).
34 S. Pattemore, *The People of God in the Apocalypse: Discourse, Structure and Exegesis* (Cambridge: Cambridge University Press, 2004).
35 J. Hollander, *The Figure of Echo: A Mode of Allusion in Milton and After* (Berkeley: University of California Press, 1981); T. M. Greene, *The Light in Troy: Imitation and Discovery in Renaissance Poetry* (New Haven, CT: Yale University Press, 1982).
36 For a recent debate on these issues among evangelical scholars, see K. Berding and J. Lunde, *Three Views on the New Testament Use of the Old Testament* (Grand Rapids, MI: Zondervan, 2007). The three views are those of Walter Kaiser, Darrell Bock and Peter Enns.
37 For a set of essays mainly from this perspective, see Porter and Stanley, *As it is Written*.

Select bibliography

This select bibliography is divided into those works that are recommended for further reading, followed by those that have been important in writing this book but are more technical (and usually much more expensive).

Further reading

Bassler, J. M., *Navigating Paul: An Introduction to Key Theological Concepts* (Louisville, KY: Westminster John Knox Press, 2007).

Das, A. A., *Paul, the Law and the Covenant* (Peabody, MA: Hendrickson, 2001).

Hays, R. B., *Echoes of Scripture in the Letters of Paul* (New Haven, CT: Yale University Press, 1989).

Hays, R. B., *The Conversion of the Imagination: Paul as Interpreter of Israel's Scripture* (Grand Rapids, MI: Eerdmans, 2005).

Holmgren, F. C., *The Old Testament and the Significance of Jesus* (Grand Rapids, MI: Eerdmans, 1999).

Moyise, S., *Evoking Scripture: Seeing the Old Testament in the New* (London and New York: T. & T. Clark, 2008).

Pietersma, A. and Wright, B. G. (eds), *New English Translation of the Septuagint* (Oxford University Press, 2007).

Porter, S. E. and Stanley, C. D. (eds), *As it is Written: Studying Paul's Use of Scripture* (Atlanta, GA: SBL, 2008).

Stanley, C. D., *Arguing with Scripture: The Rhetoric of Quotations in the Letters of Paul* (New York and London: T. & T. Clark, 2004).

Stegemann, H., *The Library of Qumran* (Grand Rapids, MI: Eerdmans, 1998).

More technical

Adeyemi, F., *The New Covenant Torah in Jeremiah and the Law of Christ in Paul* (Frankfurt am Main: Peter Lang, 2006).

Albl, M. C., *'And Scripture Cannot be Broken': The Form and Function of Early Christian Testimonia Collections* (Leiden: Brill, 1999).

Belleville, L. L., *Reflections of Glory: Paul's Polemical Use of the Moses–Doxa Tradition in 2 Corinthians 3.1–18* (Sheffield: JSOT Press, 1991).

Select bibliography

Berkley, T. W., *From a Broken Covenant to Circumcision of the Heart: Pauline Intertextual Exegesis in Romans 2.17–29* (SBLDS 175; Atlanta, GA: SBL, 2000).

Ciampa, R. E., *The Presence and Function of Scripture in Galatians 1 and 2* (WUNT, 2.102; Tübingen: Mohr Siebeck, 1998).

Dunn, J. D. G., *The Theology of Paul the Apostle* (Edinburgh: T. & T. Clark, 1998).

Ellis, E. E., *Paul's Use of the Old Testament* (Edinburgh: Oliver & Boyd, 1957).

Evans, C. A. and Sanders, J. A. (eds), *Paul and the Scriptures of Israel* (Sheffield: JSOT Press, 1993).

Goppelt, L., *Typos: The Typological Interpretation of the Old Testament in the New* (Grand Rapids, MI: Eerdmans, 1982).

Hafemann, S. J., *Paul, Moses, and the History of Israel: The Letter/Spirit Contrast and the Argument from Scripture in 2 Corinthians 3* (Carlisle: Paternoster, 2005).

Hanson, A. T., *Studies in Paul's Technique and Theology* (London: SPCK, 1974).

Hays, R. B., *The Faith of Jesus Christ: An Investigation of the Narrative Substructure of Galatians 3:1—4:11* (2nd edn; Grand Rapids, MI: Eerdmans, 2002).

Heil, J. P., *The Rhetorical Role of Scripture in 1 Corinthians* (Atlanta, GA: SBL, 2005).

Hübner, H., *Law in Paul's Thought* (Edinburgh: T. & T. Clark, 1984).

Keesmaat, S. C., *Paul and his Story: (Re)Interpreting the Exodus Tradition* (JSNTSup 181; Sheffield: Sheffield Academic Press, 1999).

Räisänen, H., *Paul and the Law* (Philadelphia: Fortress Press, 1986).

Wagner, J. R., *Heralds of the Good News: Isaiah and Paul 'In Concert' in the Letter to the Romans* (Leiden: Brill, 2002).

Watson, F., *Paul and the Hermeneutics of Faith* (London: T. & T. Clark, 2004).

Wright, N. T., *The Climax of the Covenant: Christ and the Law in Pauline Theology* (Edinburgh: T. & T. Clark, 1991).

Index of biblical references

Index of biblical references

Index of authors and subjects